Finding Male Sexuality

A Personal Journey in Awakening the Masculine Sexual Self

Carl E. Stevens, Jr.

Second edition

ISBN: 978-0-9801663-5-4
Self-As-Source Publishing

Author: Carl E. Stevens, Jr.
Published: June 2013

Consultant: Amtchat Edwards

Original Title Inspired by Toi Shanice DeVaughn

Web Address: http://www.jujumama.com

JUJUMAMA

DEDICATION

This book is dedicated to the two foundational women in my life; my wife, Kenya K. Stone-Stevens, who has traveled with me for a millennia helping me come into my higher consciousness; and my life partner, Crystal Marie George, who has demonstrated unconditional love and helped me become whole once again.

CONTENTS

CONTENTS

FOREWORD

MEN TODAY ARE AT a sexual and relationships crossroads. The choice is to continue to live your relationship and sexual life according to the standard narrative of relating, which is an extension of the pseudo-patriarchal and troubadour-based romanticism, or to acknowledge how we really feel and what we really want and move towards our sexual and relationship potential. The choice is to take a stand in saving our families, children, communities, and ultimately our country and the world, or to continue contributing to a system and mode of behavior that spirals us downward toward moral ruin.

This book is about selected parts of my personal journey to unknowingly expand my sexual awareness and sense of self. It's about how my socially accepted expectations of male sexuality prevented me from having completely fulfilling sexual experiences for much of my adult life, and how these same expectations prevented me from understanding the women I interacted with. After being introduced to the art of tantra and sacred sexuality, I found myself being opened to deeper and deeper encounters with my lovers. These deep encounters became lessons that I would incorporate into my sexual and relationship life going forward.

You'll find that I've been quite candid as I detail my experiences with the magical women in my life and the transformations that occurred during my sexual encounters with each of them. I've tried to be vulnerable, yet forthcoming with how I actually felt during these encounters with the goal being to give other men permission to do the same. Even though I didn't know what I was doing most times with women, I still felt an air of arrogance about myself. Then there were other times I felt fearful and ashamed when it wasn't at all called for.

We all think highly of ourselves when it comes to certain areas of life and, in turn, have our doubts about our skills and abilities in other areas. Wherever you are in your life is where you are and the only important thing is where we go from here.

The one commonality in the stories I tell is my deep connectedness to the women I was with. I actually believe that it's more natural to have deep connections with multiple people throughout your life than not to. The more we can feel these connections the more we'll be able to love in general and have compassion for others. The more deep connections we have the less egocentric we become with a greater willingness to give and sacrifice for others and not just ourselves. So, yes, I was deeply connected to these women and I hold their presence in my life as something highly sacred and with great respect and gratitude.

These lessons literally saved my life and greatly benefitted the lives of my partners and hopefully, you can benefit in the same way. It's never too late to begin your sexual journey as a man on this planet and there's always something else to learn and experience. Stay open to the possibilities and stay hungry for personal growth and development.

This book is written in two parts:

- PART 1 – detailed sexual encounters and relationship experiences I've had with women I've dated over the past few years and the sexual lessons and realizations resulting from those experiences.
- PART 2 – gives information and techniques that men can use to improve their sexual potency and awareness.

FOREWORD

PREFACE

WHAT'S BETTER THAN SOME raw, butt ass naked sex? No, really. I can't think of anything. There have been times in my life when I would say food sometimes gives sex a strong run for its money, but not really. Other times, I would say maybe hanging out with friends with plenty of drinks, Dominican cigars, a money knot, and plenty of time on our hands. But even that doesn't amount to much without topping the evening off with some pussy. Sometimes I forget how good sex is until I'm square in between two smooth wide open legs with painted toes hugging my torso. That's when I remember there is nothing on earth that comes close and all material gratification pales in comparison. I'm not saying one hundred million in the bank wouldn't feel good as hell, but best believe, some of that money would be used to position me nicely to get some of the most premier nani the planet has ever witnessed. I mean, money's only purpose is to obtain material items anyway, of which nani could be classified as one in many people's opinion.

And when I say butt naked raw that's exactly what I mean. That's no plastic bag or no pull out timing method, only back to the Creator raw-style lovemaking. Yes! Other fucking is good too, but it doesn't compare to the butt naked raw-style and I know I'm right. People get married so they can have the raw, no-think, no-guilt, no-regret sex. Betty White said she got married so she could have sex. My wife Kenya K said she's wanted to be married since age fourteen because she wanted to have sex and it be legal; meaning, accepted by society. This is a big deal for women especially, who have the greatest desire to have sex, but are judged the heaviest for having it. I remember hearing a lecture by Dick Gregory when I was in graduate school and he mentioned how good raw sex was and I was thinking, he's overblowing this big time. I had done some good fucking by that age, or so I thought, anyway. But twenty years later, I realized he was right and I hadn't really been having raw butt-naked sex. Up till then, sex had been fear-based sex – fear of pregnancy, of STDs, of heartbreak, of embarrassment, of criticism, and most of all, fear of feeling fully. It wasn't a free flow, thoughtless activity to heal and uplift. I didn't start having that type of sex until my late thirties. It's so funny because I can see men reading this now with thirty years of fucking under their belts thinking they got the sex thing on lock down. It's so hard to tell men stuff, especially about the big subjects – politics, women, sexuality, career, religion, etc. Men swear they know every damn thing. What a waste. My dad used to tell me you don't know shit until you atleast hit fifty and even then you're just scratching the surface. I used to think I knew so much about sex when I really didn't know shit, but over time I began to learn. Over time I began to open up and discover myself and feel. I met a Tantric guru named Shantam Nityama and a whole new world was opened up to me and the journey began for me, again.

I remember when I was dating the Tantric Goddess after I opened up my marriage. She had an appreciation and love for sex in all its forms. One night when we were driving back from somewhere, I don't even remember at this point, but it was clear we weren't going to make it back to the condo because it was at least ten minutes away or something unreasonable like that. We were in Buckhead, an upper-class neighborhood of Atlanta where spectacular houses are surrounded by aged trees, landscaped yards and expensive cars. I remember driving and looking over at her and her eyes were speaking to me. She damn near broke me all the way down with those beautiful eyes. I can still hear them speaking to me to this day.

Eyes of the Tantric Goddess: "*Rakhem. I really need you to pull this car over and fuck this pussy like it stole every gift you've ever received for your birthday and Christmas from childhood till now. I need you to do this because it hurts. It's hurting me baby and I need you to defeat her, to tame her, to remind her why your cock is so essential to me living my best life. There's no time. I have about sixty seconds before my pussy explodes into a thousand pieces and falls into an abyss for all eternity. I need your big hard cock so badly. Please pull this motherfucker over, be my Soldier, and march up into this pussy George Patton style. Please."*

After I recovered from her hypnotic eyes, I could now feel the urgency in my soul. This was a matter of National Security equivalent to our borders being invaded by the Dark Lord. I found the first side-cut I could. It wasn't even a driveway, but more like a ten-foot dirt patch leading up to a fence right off of a back road. Usually, I'm pretty good about finding a "bone" spot for some car action. I can get really creative with it, but this was a hack job at best. Like if anyone drove by they would say to themselves, "That looks like two people fucking in a car." But this wasn't even a back seat episode. Next thing I know, I have the Tantric Goddess on the trunk of the car with her dress pulled up, her thick-ass legs hanging off the car loosely embracing mine, high heels tapping the bumper like a kindergartner playing the xylophone, both her arms propping her body up, and her eyes dead locked on mine saying, "*You made the right decision Rakhem. You're doing the right thing Rakhem.*" When I looked down at her feet and saw toe rings and painted nails my dick got even harder, if that's even possible. Like bust out the skin harder.

Normally when I would slide my penis inside of her it would take some effort just because our cock-to-pussy ratio wasn't optimal for entry. But tonight I found the magic or the angle or something and slid my cock right into the wettest pussy in Buckhead, guaranteed. Moments like this are not conscious for me, meaning I'm not fully present because I'm partly in my head and partly in a slight state of trance. So because I'm often in a state of trance during sex, I have these periods where I wake up and proceed to take note of my current circumstance. It's like my Zen moment. In my Zen moment that night, I remembered thinking about what a beautiful night it was. I could see the stars and hear those cricket motherfuckers in the background. You know the ones you can never see, but it sounds like there are ten thousand of those fuckers all around you screeching those legs. It's like, just go ahead and take over the planet now cricket bugs! What are you waiting for? You've obviously got us all surrounded and you can see us, but we can't see you!

The night air was perfect. The Creator had enough mercy upon me to give me a slight cool breeze across my face to prevent me from going blind from excessive perspiration. I could hear the Tantric Goddess calling my name and moaning with ecstasy. By this time her consciousness had gone to a far away land or another galaxy. She was dancing with the angels and they were singing her praise; touching her, loving her, whispering to her about the secrets of the Universe, and introducing her to her entire ancestral lineage. They were taking away the pain and giving her the tools and power to create her best life all in that moment. I could see it with my own eyes and feel it with my own energy. I also noticed I was in one of the most awkward positions a man could be in while fucking. I was leaning backward off of her so she could lie on the trunk comfortably and so I could support her ass and legs. My knees were slightly bent because this was a little car and I'm at least six foot three. To top it off, I was standing on this gravel/dirt combination so leverage was about two on a scale of one to ten. But you know how it is during ecstasy, right? There's no stopping, no adjusting, none of that, because it will break the rhythm and breaking the rhythm means snapping her out of trance and bringing her back to earth. I just couldn't do that. The only option I had was to zone back out and come to consciousness at a later time. Otherwise I wouldn't have made it. Of course, none of this is about me cumming. As a matter of fact, I didn't orgasm that night. I knew in that moment the only thing stopping us from fucking until Christmas was my fitness level. That's the question. When will Rakhem's legs buckle under the pressure? When will he listen to the voice in his head?

Inner Voice in my head: *"Fuck this, Holmes. Let's go get some sleep. What's the benefit to us man? Just answer me that question. I mean I know you love the girl, but you bought her dinner, had a great time, you all fucked before you left and you damn near threw your back out in that session. Let's call it a night and live to see another day."*

That's the same voice that tells you it's alright to stop at two miles instead of three during your morning jog.

So I went away to a place so my body could do its thing. When I came back the night was still beautiful, the Tantric Goddess was still appreciative and I decided to listen to the voice, but not till she was totally satiated and the pussy was tamed. The entire experience with her was beautiful, but what I loved more was the sincere appreciation she showed me for loving her the way she wanted in that very moment. It made it all worthwhile. I also loved the look of,

"What the fuck Rakhem?! You gave me another experience to remember forever. Thank you. I love you."

That night I had the chance to practice going beyond pain and personal preference and allowed my will to be subjected to her desire. For the year of life she allowed me to share with her,

17

the Tantric Goddess helped me learn the power of subjecting my will. I discuss this lesson in the chapter, *The Tantric Goddess*. She also taught me to go beyond myself and find the pleasure in the pain. I discuss this lesson in the chapter, *A Sadomasochistic Friend Indeed*.

PREFACE

INTRODUCTION

INTRODUCTION

WHEN I LOOK BACK at my life, I know it's been a journey towards something very specific, but obvious ignorance in the present, combined with hindsight, has proven I've had absolutely no idea what that specific thing is. When I say no idea, I really do mean none whatsoever. You really don't know what's going on until years after the fact, even when everything seems to be going according to plan. I remember the elders, specifically my dad and one of my spiritual teachers, telling me I wouldn't begin understanding what life was all about until I hit fifty years old. Before that, anything you're thinking can be pretty much discarded. That is how my sexual journey has been. I thought I really understood sex. I remember like yesterday when I was in college during my late teens and early twenties, knowing I was the fucking man when it came to laying it down. Then I hit my late twenties and realized I was on the kindergarten level back then. When I hit my late twenties, I started learning about sexual alchemy, which is the science of how to manipulate your sexual energy. I learned skills, like controlling my ejaculation during sex and what to do with the energy I saved and accumulated. I learned there were certain times of the day, month, and year that were best for intercourse as well as how diet and energy work (chi gong, etc.) played into the quality of my sexual experience. I learned that I could somehow combine my partner and I's sexual energy and use it to create actual material things. Then something miraculous happened, I hit my late thirties. It was then I learned that I didn't know shit about the female anatomy, her orgasmic potential or mine. I didn't know shit about an orgasm actually; what it was, how it was generated, why it happened, or any of that. I didn't know a woman could ejaculate fluid out of her urethra during sex or that she could have a full body orgasm that looked eerily similar to someone having a seizure or that I could bring a woman to an orgasmic plateau without even touching her. I would say one of the biggest things I've learned during this time was my identity as a sexual being. I learned what I did and didn't like when it came to sex and not just positions here, but the fact that I really enjoyed the energetic exchange with my partner more than the physical exchange. I learned the love I sought in others was really me looking to honor and love the part of me those people represented. I learned that sharing is impossible where guilt, shame, victimization, and lack of self worth existed and that what I thought was sharing was actually taking, covering up, and running from myself. I learned that vulnerability, stillness, and the subtlest of energy is the key to your personal freedom and power and that we all have a masculine and feminine aspect to our being which demands expression and a voice in our life.

All I can say is if the elders were right, fifty is going to be a doozy.

♠

This book is for open-minded individuals looking to expand their experience around sex and intimacy and those who are just interested in my sexual and tantric journey during the first few years of my open relationship. If you're a close-minded person (it may be tough to admit this, but look deep inside), super religious (as in, the world is going to end very soon and most folks are going to hell, but you'll ascend to heaven), self-realized (already knows it all), on a higher consciousness level (already knows it all), self-righteous (everyone else is basically wrong), or unfulfilled (pissed, angry, sad, depressed with consistency throughout your life) and looking for something outside of yourself to complain about in order to feel more accomplished and worthy of living, feel free to put the book down now. It's not for you. Well, actually the book is for you, but you're probably not open enough to receive it. See how much time I saved you?

This book is about my sexual evolution and a part of my journey into a higher sexual consciousness. Quite often, I refer to tantra in this book, but I don't consider what I do to be exactly tantra. What I focus on is Sexual Alchemy. That is, how sexuality can be used as a transformative process to shape our individual and collective lives. Tantra is a formalized practice around sex, but its original focus was changed to be predominately about men and their sexual work. The origins of tantra were practiced by earlier civilizations that were more advanced than the originators of tantra as we know it today. From my experience both women and men need to understand their potential as sexual beings. Many of the principles I believe in and practice do coincide with tantra, but right now, I am talking about evolving the sexual practice to improve our life and the lives of others on earth.

Also, this is not a how-to textbook on Sexual Alchemy or Tantric sex. If you are looking for a step-by-step guide to doing tantra, there are a myriad of books on the market.

The approach I have taken here is a raw uncut guy approach. I need to just tell it how it is, which includes how I was feeling during my encounters with the various women throughout this time in my life. To do so, I am choosing to tell a series of individual stories and show how certain experiences increased the awareness of my own sexuality. I say raw because it's a no-holds-barred description of my encounters along with the lessons I've learned as a result. Additionally, I'm not trying to be politically correct here. In this case I believe as much realism as possible is needed to fully convey my feelings during each episode. For example, I wasn't going around having intercourse with various women, but making love or straight fucking. I was never looking forward to some vagina, but most definitely some wet pussy.

Ready Set Go!

The first time I had sex I was fucking so fast you would think someone was standing over me with a stopwatch. Like it was the Fuck Fast OlympicsTM and I was going for the world speed record. I was going for an average of eighty pumps a minute for ten minutes to become the new world champion. Oh, and stamina is no problem at age seventeen. At that age you can run or pump for six days straight without breaking a sweat. Plus, you're so excited to be square in some pussy you can't feel anything anyway. The whole time I was pumping all I could think about was telling the fellas all about it. I would finally be free of the mental torture of being a virgin and having to listen to all the guys talk about the plethora of sex they were having every day after basketball practice. My options were to lose my virginity or just slit my wrists and that wasn't really an option because the rest of life was so much fun.

Oh yeah, plus, the girls like that, right? When you are pumping a mile a minute making them scream like Tom Cruise when he did his girlfriend in *Jerry Maguire*. I mean she said it, "Don't ever stop fucking me!" Ok, I have my marching orders. Long, hard, and forever is what the girls want. Jerry didn't seem to enjoy himself too much, but the lady was clear on what she wanted.

So my work was cut out for me right away. My impression of what sex was and what women liked was shaped by Jerry Maguire's girlfriend, TV, and my peers who were basically lying and clueless.

This would be the first set of information I would have to upload out of my consciousness as I began to learn about Sexual Alchemy.

Car Love

Fucking in the backseat of a car is the dopeness. Let's not even play around with that one. I mean, that's what I heard from my friends who told me about it. It's the best way to keep it real when it comes to connecting sexually with someone. I'm not talking about getting head in the front seat of the Hummer with tinted windows. Where's the risk in that? You may as well be in your room at the house with the door closed. I'm talking about fucking in the back seat of a hooptie pulled behind a trash dumpster in an alley at three-thirty in the morning, straight banging in the back seat. It's really about bringing your 'A' game. It's a close proximity hand-to-hand combat of the highest kind. Like a WWF cage match or getting a piece when you've been locked up in solitary confinement for a month. We're not talking about making love here, which is the silk sheets at the house scenario with candles, background music, incense, and fresh towels. Humping is about as close to making love in the back seat as you're going to get, but bucking and grinding are probably better verbs. It's just nothing nice. Everything's got to be in order. No bathroom. No mouthwash. You've got to go with what you got! Lights! Camera! Action!

I lost my virginity in a car. Well, technically anyway. If you cum before you put the condom on, but still get the penis inside the vagina does that count? Ok, well, yeah, I lost mine in the back seat of my orange AMC Spirit. For men reading this who are over forty, you may have forgotten about the days when you could cum and shoot off like a hose and still be hard as diamonds. The biggest thing I remember about those days is sex didn't feel like much.

I mean it felt good, but not as good as cumming at twenty. And twenty didn't have shit on thirty and thirty is really light weight compared to forty. I'll get back to you in ten years on what fifty feels like, but I've got my hopes up. Actually, it's almost guaranteed it will feel better than forty if the past twenty years are any indication. My older brother used to say the later years were good and he wasn't joking. I still remember him saying thirty was the shit when I was twenty-three. I was like, "*Take that shit somewhere else Holmes.*" Twenty-three is the shiznit. I felt like Zeus in this bitch. I was in awesome shape, had a big ass dick, was fucking everyday, looked good, and the girls were stuck to my jock like scotch tape on poster board.

But fucking in a car is the dopeness because of the circumstances and environment as opposed to just the sex itself per se. Feel me? If you're fucking in a car it's because you don't have a place or don't have time to go to a place or because you and home girl shouldn't be fucking in the first place or the desire is so strong there's no time to get back to the house. And it's not just the fucking that's dope, but even the preamble. How many of you have had the pleasure of driving around trying to find that perfect spot at three in the morning? I've found that the best place is usually in public or out in the open, but women want you to find a fucking bat cave in order to feel safe and secure. The only exception is when they're ovulating. Then they're like, "*Just pull this motherfucker over and absolutely murder this pussy.*"

You don't even have to be in the car, it's just something about being near a car or on it. I had sex with the Tantric Goddess (future chapter) against her car and that shit was dope as hell. It was so live that even though I couldn't breathe and I was so tired, it felt like both lungs were going to collapse and I started going blind. I couldn't stop fucking because there's just something about raw fucking on a car outside with birds, squirrels and crickets staring at your ass. I remember having sex with my ex-girlfriend in broad daylight in the middle of a heavily traveled walkway while leaning against a car. It was winter so I had a long Triple Fat Goose coat on to cover things up. But still, who would suspect someone would be fucking in broad daylight in the most public place on campus? That's where the extreme rush comes from. And that's cool. But, throughout my tantric journey I began to get these same types of rushes from the variations of sex I was having. It was the quality and approach to the sex, mixed with the rush and intense feelings. There's a difference. When you can't find the specialness and intensity in the act itself, you begin to look for things to make it more intense and exciting; like hanging off of a chandelier or choking the shit out of your partner or hanging from the ceiling by your nut sack. Believe me, I'm not knocking what people do for excitement or pleasure. The sky's the limit as far as I'm concerned and as long as you're cool with it, I am too. For me, it was critical I find the deeper aspects of sex within the act itself. Why? Because I would go into healing women and educating men about the possibility of getting the most from the sexual experience and connecting to your partner to facilitate closeness. So I would have to come up with more than hanging off the ceiling by the hairs on your nut sack or jumping off the roof face first into the pussy or wear a clown costume as a solution for expanding the couple's experience with sex; although, I'm sure some of my clients would love for me to say that.

Beta Test

Women, most of your relationship problems stem from the fact that you are dating Beta and Gamma men. Well, obviously, it's the part of your personality and character, which attracts you to that type of man (read *Change Your Man* by Kenya K. Stevens for details), but let's discount your issues for a minute. What I mean is you are dating men who didn't start getting consistent pussy until they were in their mid-to-late twenties or later. These men had little to no natural sex appeal and therefore didn't attract women into their lives. They were mainly masturbating through their first ten to twenty years of sexual maturity and weren't too happy about that. As a result, they are punishing your ass and you don't even know it. But I'm not going to let the women off the hook here. There are Beta and Gamma women out there too. Beta women are the ones who damn near had zero sex appeal themselves, but had an interest in being with Alpha men. Gamma women have zero sex appeal and little interest in being with a man or anyone. They often find alternatives to dealing with their sensual and relationship desires like excessive church activities, career, or something that hides them from the public eye.

You know, it's four in the morning, the club is clear and I'm in the parking lot absolutely refusing to jack off tonight, but still that Long Island Ice Tea is talking much shit to me. It's saying, "*Looks don't matter when the lights go out, we can use mouthwash for the breath issue, and no worries, you don't have to give her your actual phone number.*" Your cock and nuts start giving you advice and direction too.

Your Cock and Nuts: "*Just wander the parking lot, I guarantee you there is something out here that we can take home TONIGHT with no questions asked. Ah, there she is, the perfect Gamma sister. And look Holmes, do not beat around the bush here. Give her one or two lines and then ask her home. After all it is four a.m. and you grabbing me with those callused hands is getting old even with the baby oil. Plus, we've been through half the porn on the web and I know most of these chicks by heart now. Shit, I practically know their social security numbers. You should be able to get with a woman on occasion, like the rest of the fellas are claiming."*

The bottom line is if you're Beta or Gamma you just need to get some skills and a new perspective. It just means you're dealing with something for which you have no experience. Before I started getting pussy on a regular basis I was basically a danger to women. I didn't know what I was doing sexually or otherwise. I didn't know how men affected women emotionally or what women wanted from men. There's nothing like learning this through experience. There's nothing like having legitimate confidence in your skills as a man. Otherwise, you will hold women accountable for your failures. It's true homie. We've all heard the victimization complaint, *"Why don't they choose me? I'm a nice guy."* LMAO. Oh boy!

But all these 'types' of men and women are relative. I was an Alpha male until the age of twenty-two or so. When I moved to Washington, DC I quickly became a Gamma male. Yep, it happens that quickly. A different environment, different folks, different criteria for attracting and relating to women will all contribute to how you're manhood is categorized. When I got to DC I had no cash, no Benz, no DC game, and no chance to get pussy on a regular basis. I might as well have moved to China or the Amazon. It was like being a freshman in college all over again. The only thing saving me was one of my tight boys lived in northern Virginia and he had a Benz, or in DC language, a pussy magnet. Yep, even for the passenger seat brothers there was play to be had until TLC released that *Scrubs* song and put me back at square one.

The problem is the Gamma and Delta men and women spend a large part of their life and energy trying to get a leg up on the dating game rather than mastering their masculinity and femininity or learning how to connect intimately with their partner. They're attempting to position themselves to be more 'attractive' to the Alpha folks. Here's the problem; it's working too often. These individuals will get the job, Benz, nice clothes, fly pad, pick up some dating tips online, watch some porno techniques, and do some basic refinements to their game without doing anything substantial to address the issues that made them Gamma and Beta males in the beginning. For a man it's a lack of knowledge of his masculine nature, sex, and life. For a woman it's a lack of understanding her feminine nature, what real power means for a women, understanding and acknowledging her true sexual nature, and her role in life. I'm sorry, but a Benz or six figure income is not going to fix it. Going to the gym to get a few muscles definitely isn't going to fix it. Your issues will come out in marriage or in dating or wherever, but the men and women you're preying on don't recognize that. They see the Benz and assume you're an Alpha male, but you're really a Gamma man in disguise, like it's Halloween or some shit. Women do this too. You buy into the illusion that if you have a degree or an advanced degree or a six figure income and a house, you are more of a woman and more attractive. The only thing you'll attract with that is either a man who just wants to hit it or a man who doesn't want to work and live off of your ass. You have to have your character and skills in order to attract the best mate. My point here is that you can't address your issues with Band-Aids. You have to do the work; that's just the reality. Doing the work will also help you stop blaming everyone else in your life for your "failures," including the Beta person you attracted. You all love to ride this guilt trip as a justification for acquiring material things to make you a better man, woman, or whatever. "*I don't need a man; I'll just do my own thing.*" Or the

30

man saying, "*I just can't find a good woman,*" which is one of the biggest bullshit lines ever created.

But here's the thing; if you have some basic skills in Sexual Alchemy and the tantric sciences and understand your masculine nature, you become Universal with your sex appeal with women. It's not so much about location and culture because you understand how you tick and you understand how to connect with a woman. And women are women. I don't care where you are on the planet. Outside of cultural traditions everything is the same underneath and knowing this is what makes you truly Alpha because you know what you can do and more importantly what needs to be done. The point is, there was a time in my life where I didn't have basic training in sex, intimacy, the science of women or anything that would have transcended time and space. I didn't get it until I delved into the alchemical sexual sciences much later in my life.

THE PRECEPT

AFTER MY WIFE AND I reconciled our sex life through tantric and other sexual alchemical exercises we began to move apart sexually once again. This was primarily due to the fact that we would both go on a journey to expand our sexual natures even though we weren't totally aware of this at the time. Retrospection seems to be as close to twenty-twenty as you can get when it comes to life unless your intuitive ability is on lock.

When I say we reconciled our sex life, I mean we were able to come together sexually in a powerful way. We learned to create and manifest through sex. We manifested cars, cash, jobs, and a new living situation for the family. It was nice to see things come to fruition through this process; still is, actually. We also manifested some major challenges and obstructions by not understanding what we were doing throughout this process. But that's what happens when you don't have a teacher leading you through alchemical processes. We started out with clues from who we both considered to be gurus in the metaphysical sciences, tied in with a heavy background in the occult sciences: meditation, ritual, trance work, etc. Everything else for us came through intuition and trial and error. That's the path of a master teacher. You agree to have some limited training in the metaphysical arts, but eventually move out on your own to uncover certain truths on your own.

Contrary to popular belief, everything is not passed down from one master to the next. It's actually the exception to the rule. If you receive the complete lesson from your master then you are not a master. You can only be the holder or messenger of the information. Masters go through major trials to obtain their knowledge and often times have numerous "life events" as a result of the raw power of what they've obtained and how they've obtained it. The rule is that most teachers must access knowledge directly from a source. It's a part of the initiation actually. Almost all people who have learned a metaphysical, occult, or alchemical science have learned from a student as opposed to a master and that's fine because most likely what you do with the information won't be impactful to the planet on a large scale; therefore, the time of a master is not required for most people.

The other piece we addressed was sexual skills, control, and discipline. I mastered not ejaculating during sex with her. She mastered having orgasm after orgasm, full body and localized, internal and squirting. We improved (not mastered by any stretch) our ability to add quality oral sex to our mix. I mastered the movement of energy during and after sex through meditation techniques, breathing exercises, eye rotations, and gathering both the internal and external alchemical agent. I felt very strong sexually; the strongest of my entire life at the ripe age of thirty-six.

But my life has never been about ease or comfort. I am not on the planet to master one technique and just chill out. I know that goes against what most people establish as their goals, but it's just not mine. My goal is self-mastery. It's not a choice it's an agreement – a contract. I receive this body with specific tools, talents, gifts and a network of celestial beings to support me in this journey in exchange for helping them in theirs and doing the work and inserting that knowledge and experience back into the space-time continuum. I'm getting all I can get during this incarnation. I've come to master life in this particular consciousness and energetic body. So once I pass one test, it's on to the next one (not by choice) as I'm moved into these new situations by spirit. I chose this life before I incarnated and I accept and embrace it.

On our sexual journey we had gone as far as we could go with each other from a learning and experimentation perspective. We could still come together for the purpose of manifestation and healing one another as that is a skill which is always needed and valued. At this point, we will definitely come together again very soon and continue the journey and expand out again I'm sure. The gods were telling us to expand out, learn and grow and so we did – we are. Enter the open relationship.

THE BACKGROUND

I AM A TANTRIC healer and practitioner amongst other things. Another job is to help women open up to their highest sexuality, sensuality, orgasmic nature, and to increase their magnetism so they may create the life they want. What does that mean? It means helping women get more from every experience in their life including sex. Helping women be present in their sexual experience allowing them to feel it fully, completely, and feeling free to respond organically without guilt, shame, or insecurity. I heal women and instruct men so they may do the same. I believe we all create our own lives. Everything taking place in our lives is our responsibility and not the responsibility of others or a god in the sky. So as I work with women, I help them increase their magnetic nature so they may attract all they desire, including their life partner or partners. It also includes the money and resources they desire and good will from others. While this process may sound complex or difficult, it's not, for all they must do is open up to what they desire. That's easy enough, right?

Most of the time, it's not very easy at all. We have forgotten how to feel in this culture. We have forgotten not only how to love and even what it is we truly love and as a result, we navigate our lives based on our conscious logical minds rather than from a place of feeling and trusting our inner voice. For women this is a sure death. When a woman does not feel, it means she is not living as herself, but as a shadow of herself. She is living in a glass case watching the world around her, but never truly experiencing it for what it is; the pain, pleasure, or peace it offers. The pain most women feel is really not from life's stimuli, but from the desire to be free and their struggles to get there. It's a discomfort of never truly knowing the depths of their soul. It is knowing something else is inside of them wanting to express itself, but having no idea how to get in touch with it. This is the source of the pain. It's not from the relationship breakup, the friendship betrayal, the lack of career fulfillment, or the lack of financial resources.

I'm in an open relationship. What that means is I don't live in a cage. It means I can be completely open and honest with myself and my wife and everyone else about how I feel and what I want. It means my wife is my partner, lover, friend, confidant, and companion – not my overseer. I can have any kind of relationship I want with anyone I want at any time. Yes, this includes sex. How did I get here? To be honest, it all feels like a dream. It feels like I was and still am on a ride – a life ride. But what it really means is I've reached a place of true freedom within myself and this freedom is reflected in my primary relationship with my wife. She is open and supportive of me in my journey and I of her in her journey.

The open marriage played seamlessly into my life's work of achieving mastery in the area of Sexual Alchemy as I've been allowed to put the practice to full motion with a number of women in the form of clients, lovers, and girlfriends. What has opened up before me is a world I would never have known. Tell me, how many experiences can you get from one source? I suppose one could have many experiences, but not nearly enough to obtain mastery of the Self. The open relationship allowed me to do what I am instructing my clients to do, which is to follow your passion, heart, and desire and live life authentically. It is to live the full experience of life and not be channeled into a path of monotony and boredom only to waste this very valuable life you've been given. These are very valuable physical, mental, and spiritual tools you've been given.

What if you left this planet without truly connecting to someone in the deepest way possible? What if you left this planet without connecting to your many soul mates on a deep sexual and spiritual level all because someone told you your nature is opposed to your sexuality – against it in some way? What if your power lies *not* in your formal education, but rather in your ability to freely, and in an unobstructed manner, channel your Source-given energy throughout every single meridian causing you to produce and create like the God you were built in the likeness of. You are the blessing, but it doesn't lie in your conformity, unless, of course, that is your gift. It lies in your expression.

Think back to when you were a child, age two or three, walking with your mom and dad through the mall or park and all you wanted to do was connect with the most interesting people all around you. The different shape, sizes and colors they displayed were nothing less than amazing. If only you could have touched her face, grabbed his nose, untied his shoes, taken a bite of her cotton candy. Experience. That's all. It's a tool to breed intelligence beyond what any textbook could ever give us. Even studying your own body in amazement. What is that? It's hanging off of my waist like an elephant's trunk or perhaps it's the vacuum between your legs feeling like something should be there as it calls you to explore it.

Throughout my marriage, eighteen years and counting at this point, I've had attractions and feelings of love for other people. The difference between then and now is I never acted on those feelings. I just kind of did the 'right' thing. Suppress those dreaded "*She's attractive and calling something inside of me*" feelings in order to maintain our monogamous union and find favor with the larger institution of society and religion; living up to our parents' expectations even though they could not do it themselves. We were doing our best to be the Cleavers and the Cosbys. Meanwhile, the actors playing these roles are in and out of relationships like dresses on the Macy's rack the Saturday before Valentine's Day. Thanks for the leadership. Thanks for being a great role model. You got me right where society wants me. After all, misery invites company, right? Suppress who you really are and be who you're expected to be. Of course, there's always a good reason. Do it for the kids. They need an example of functional suppression and general unhappiness. Show them how to fit the fuck in. This is some bullshit. Oops, I cursed.

A favorite quote of mine sums this up nicely. It's from the movie *Spanglish* where Adam Sandler's character, John Clansky, is about to kiss his Mexican housekeeper Flor, played by Paz Vega. He kisses her and five seconds into it, Flor stops him and says they can't do this because he is married. John responds by saying, "I know, I know. We can't do anything that brings us any kind of satisfaction or release." This quote seems to sum up the situation most people find themselves in where they can't explore the things in life they are drawn to out of fear or conformity. Am I saying conformity is bad? Of course not, especially, when it makes sense. That being said, like many things in our culture, we take things to the extreme and conform so much, we forget who we are and what we like.

Have you ever had a battle with the voices in your head? It's funny to me when people try to tell me God is not inside of them. If He is not inside of me then tell me who I'm talking to? Who am I debating with? And don't chuckle cynically at me, saying, "*Ha ha. There goes another nutcase. Hey honey! Check out this guy. He's talking to himself. Cuckoo for Coco Puffs. Ha ha. Can you believe it? And he has the nerve to write a book and actually admit it. Poor guy.*"

Hmm. Should I have pizza or a burger tonight. Well I had a steak last night so I'll do pizza. This is my critic '*thinking*' to himself after dogging me to his wife. Talking to himself? Hmm…

Excuse me sir? Who are you consulting with on what to have for dinner tonight? It's just you, right? So there can't be a debate or sides, or differing views. If it's only you, then there is only one desire, one voice, one opinion, and one point of view, right? There really shouldn't be a conversation in your head. I know this is commonly accepted and not looked at as anything except normal thought processing, but in reality, it's a conversation between two or more entities or consciousnesses; two voices inside of you. I'll let that marinate, and meditation on the subject will reveal some interesting realities of our mental makeup.

That's actually a sidebar. No need to prove that we are a community in and of ourselves. As above, so below. I like to say, as within, so without. I think that's closer to what the ancients really meant.

My name is Rakhem Seku (*pronounced* rah kem • say koo). *Ra* as in the Sun God *Ra,* and Khem as in the correct name for ancient Egypt – *Khemit*. My name is Khemetic and it means, "*He who follows the wisdom of the Imperishable Ones.*" A Khemetic priest gave the name to me when I joined a spiritual society while getting my MBA at Howard University. The name sounds cool, but it actually comes with a lot of pressure and responsibility. I mean, I have to live up to it. I have to follow the wisdom of the Imperishable Ones. Who are they? They are the ones who have transcended this earthly time space reality, not once, but many times. They are the ones who understand the secrets of the universe and sail upon the waves of natural and universal law without the least bit of effort. What's in a name? A name is supposed to have meaning, and for me, it is a reminder of who you are and how you are supposed to live your life.

Sexual Phases of Man

I've gone through a number of sexual phases throughout my brief manhood. The first phase was what I called the Experience phase. I just needed to have sex at any cost because I was getting verbally pounded by other males who were claiming to have sex all the time. My self-confidence and esteem were diminishing with every story they told. Little did I know that what they were saying was mostly bullshit.

Bullshitter #1: "Yeah man. I was like fucking this girl for three hours last night. I busted like six nuts." *I'm thinking how do you bust six nuts? That sounds so exhausting.*

Bullshitter #2: "That's what's up homie. Man, last night, I was with three girls. I was doing them at the same time until I just got bored and watched them do each other." *This dude must have three dicks or something. How do you screw three girls at a time? Trying to figure that out was harder than working a 20x20 Sudoku puzzle.*

Bullshitter #3: "Ah, shit. I need to try that one. Yo, check this out, I was working the drive-through window last night and this girl ordered some fries and shit. When she pulled up she asked me to pull my shit out. So I did and she sucked it right through the drive-through window for like five minutes. I was like this is some of that old freaky-type shit." *See if that was me I would be fired instantly. Actually, I wouldn't because I know for a fact I don't have the balls to get my joint sucked through the drive-through window while I'm working. But that would be kind of live now that I think about it. I wonder did he bust a nut? Or better yet, did she get her food?*

Bullshitter #4: "Yo, you remember Jessica, right? Holmes, after basketball practice I showered up and opened my locker and yo. Jessica was crouched down, lodged in my locker Holmes. I was like, what the fuck is this shit? She told me to be quiet and just shove my dick in her mouth. Man that was the best head ever. I came so hard I thought I was gonna put a hole in the back of her throat."

Me: *Oh shit, it's my turn. Think quick.* "Um, yeah. Yeah, what happened was there were these girls and they stopped by my house because they lived in the neighborhood and the one girl was like, we are super horny. So I was like 'Oh, okay. Would you nice girls like to come in?' and they did and I fucked all of them. It was great."

As you can see my story was shaky at best. At least the bullshitters were watching porno movies or something to come up with great story lines. Their stuff flowed. Everything I said was choppy and an obvious lie. The Experience phase began at the age of seventeen and lasted for a couple of years.

The second was the Experimentation phase in which getting pussy was no longer the issue, but maximizing my efficiency was. I was interested in being with certain types of women and trying new things. For example, I wanted to see if I could fuck for four hours straight (like for real). Or how long I could eat some pussy before my tongue and jaw locked up. I also wanted to get some of that freaky-deaky on and popping, like the girls who licked assholes and sucked toes.

The third phase was the beginning of a Self-Mastery phase. This is where I learned to control my ejaculation and make this last longer, or how can I give this women a whole slew of orgasms? That had more to do with discipline and control as well as picking up certain skills that I either hadn't been exposed to up to that point or hadn't yet practiced.

The fourth phase was a Release and Surrender phase where I took my mind out of the act and was just in the moment with no emotions of fear or regret, etc. To me this is where I experienced the raw organic feeling and essence of sex during the act itself. If you're thinking or strategizing too much then you're not really in the experience. You're not experiencing sex; you're controlling it.

PART I:

The Journey

CHAPTER 1

THE BEST PUSSY ON THE PLANET

The key to the greatest enjoyment is not in the thing itself, but inside of you. It's your ability to be open and vulnerable to each experience such that its truth can be felt through the core of your soul. The sooner you understand this fact, the more fulfilling your life will be.

SOMETIMES YOU HAVE TO give yourself permission to feel and enjoy life. I know it seems to be a 'no-brainer', but I've often found myself just thinking through life and being more focused on what people think of me rather than just enjoying the moment and feeling good about myself. This is especially true in my sexual life where I've always tried to hold myself to some imaginary male standard, until I realized I am the standard and just being me is the only true requirement in life.

♠

So we've all had the experience where we get up from some raw butt naked sex and tell ourselves it was pretty much the best pussy in the country or at least the East Coast or in Texas or some shit. Good God Almighty! I mean, that was just the best nani I've ever had. My first official relationship in my open marriage journey was just that. The beautiful woman I was dating had the best pussy on the planet. It felt like a thousand angels stroking my joint with avocado lotion laden silk tissues and fresh one hundred percent cotton swabs so softly and gently as to stroke each nerve ending individually. I know right? Every position was diggity dope as hell: missionary, doggy, bottoms, side-swipers, small package, huckle-buck, back breaker, dick rider, chandelier hanger, what-the-fuck ever. It was that whip a brother until he's blind nani. That, what the fuck day is it or where did I park my car type of dopeness. No, it was the let me fix you breakfast, gourmet style with fresh fruit garnishes type of dopeness. What I'm trying to say is the pussy was good.

Let it be known I was very much attracted to this woman. She carried herself with grace and fluidity, like poetry in motion. I love women who are filled out in all the right places and carry their weight like an angelic ballerina dancing through the clouds. There's nothing sexier on the planet. She had long natural hair that was fluid like her curves. Her skin was light caramel-colored and smoother than a baby's ass after a warm bath and fresh coconut lotion rub down session with grandma. Plus, she was reserved in speech to the point where you just know she's got this wisdom thing working. She's just observing what's going on around her without saying too much, but learning all the while. I'm really into that kind of thing with women because you can ask them a bunch of questions and they have this deep penetrating insight. It adds a whole different dimension to the relationship and the conversation is captivating and can go an hour or longer without feeling like it.

Me: "*So what did you think of the dude with the blue jacket? Is he paid out?*"

She: "*No he was just fronting. I saw him triple checking the bill when his girlfriend went to the restroom. He wants to be Top Dog, but he's got a long way to go. Plus, his shoes were scuffed up.*"

It's also sexy as hell when a woman doesn't say much because it helps them exude this confidence like my words are valuable and don't come cheaply or I'm doing my research, so don't bother me.

So this was a bona-fide attraction and logically it would make perfect sense that I was intensely into her sexually in the biggest of ways. But the important thing was not that it was the best in and of itself, but why it was the best. I mean, did she really have the best pussy on the planet or is something else happening? Maybe it was a combination of things, but on one level it can be said it was the best because I was open to receiving and allowing myself to truly experience us coming together sexually. Meaning, I wasn't in a thinking, controlling mindset like I had been for most of my sexual and adult life, but a receiving mindset. I allowed myself to be completely in the experience as opposed to controlling it. The only thing I can attribute it to was being ready to receive pleasure and truly feel. This was the journey I was on, the receive-and-feel journey, because up to this point I was on the give-don't-worry-how-it-feels-because-the-nut-was-assured journey. After being introduced to tantra as a sexual art I was on the master-the-self-and-go-beyond-the-physical-feeling journey.

Inside each of us is an intuitive sense. I'll explain later how this worked in this case, but it was huge for me. I met D-Train on a cruise when I was living in the Atlanta area. I had been in an open relationship for about six months, but had not been in an official relationship to this point, only a few near misses and bad communications.

I was on a family vacation with my immediate family. Up to that point it had been pretty straight and narrow with watching and feeding kids and doing the family dinner thing. One night I was in the club on the ship checking out the scene. My wife and I had been in there the night before and it was average at best, but the only real adult thing happening on the ship. So we went back the next night to chill out. We were about half-way done on a week cruise at that point when I saw the all time thickest completely cock diesel female I had ever seen before, at least, within recent memory. Who knows if she was actually the dopest, but I've never seen anyone roll like she did on a dance floor. She was like the waves of the ocean. The thickest ass and legs with a slow sensual roll on the dance floor and what was crazy was the first night I saw her she wasn't even dressed. She was wearing black sweat pants, a t-shirt, and flip-flops in the club. Now that's confidence, roll up in the club with flip-flops and sweat pants and all the other females are wearing skirts, heels, and dresses. I got on the floor and danced with her. I didn't ask her, but just stepped up to her. She was dancing alone or with some females. After the dance, I gave her my card and asked her to call me. I saw her throughout the cruise and we had the chance to talk here and there. I'm sure she wanted to have sex with me even though she was cool as a cucumber with it, but no one had a free room. Either way we had enough time to talk on the cruise for a bit. When we hit the shore she sent me a text, which was the all time best feeling. Her area code was "404." Yes, she lived in the Atlanta area near me. Needless to say we hooked up in short order.

The first time I went to her house, we had sex. But, it wasn't just sex, it was making love without a doubt. The penis to vagina ratio was perfect. I was only slightly larger than what her vagina was built for, which is nothing that wouldn't correct itself over time. Remember those rolls she was doing on the dance floor? She moved the same way in bed. I felt I was back on that cruise ship. Luckily she rolled slow and steady otherwise she would have tossed my ass right out the window or at least onto the floor next to the bed. She was immediately feeling my cock upon entry and came soon after I entered her. We made love for about an hour and a half and we both felt every second. I finally came and pulled out because of course I was going raw style. We laid together on our backs without saying much. I remember it like yesterday. She was on my right side and my right arm was under her neck and shoulders. I didn't feel tired and my penis was soft after cumming very strong. I had one of those spinal cord nuts where you can feel the energy and spinal fluid moving down your spine into your anus, then into your nut sack, do a couple of circular twirls then shoot like a missile out the shaft of my penis. Whewww! Nice.

Here's what happened next. After laying there for about three or four minutes, I instinctively lifted her up with my right arm and put her on top of me. I didn't do that because my dick was hard again. I did it because something told me to do it. I had no idea what I was doing because to be honest I'd never done it before. Usually before I make a strong sexual move towards a woman I'm already rock-hard or at least on the way. The other part of it was after busting a nut I was good and really had zero desire to have any more sex. Actually, generally, my challenge after cumming was remembering why I was even with this woman. That wasn't the case with D-Train, but I've experienced this type of thing throughout my younger adulthood years. It's like I wouldn't only ejaculate semen, but my memory right along with it, so I had an internal conversation with myself.

Me (after ejaculating, in my head, of course): *Okay, why is this girl in my house again and what exactly did I see in her? What do I do to get out of this?*

That's how it really felt and a lot of women don't understand it. Men have memory loss after sex to the affect of "*Who are you?*"

Now recovery after sex was a whole different thing. Even in my younger days I would wait at least thirty minutes before attempting to do a round two and to be honest, I rarely did round twos. I just didn't. I guess I wasn't a potent man like that. After I nutted I was going to sleep and that's it, unless the girl insisted or wanted more, in which case, I would oblige. I could usually get back into it if I needed to or the girl could give me head and I'd be back in the game, but in the past twelve years, it wasn't a part of my sexual experience.

So, I rolled her on top of me and my dick immediately got rock hard again; like age sixteen, seven in the morning cock-so-stiff-you-can't-sleep kind of hard. Like, this is our-first-time-fucking-and-I-want-you-oh-so-bad hard. One thing women don't realize is, a man's dick can get so hard it hurts like shit. It will wake you up out of your sleep and have you pacing around the house, which is rough because even walking hurts in this state. The bad thing is nothing comforts it except wet pussy. I've tried other alternatives like a cold shower, sticking it in a bucket of water, letting it air out, or whatever. I think that's why teenagers masturbate so much; not because they are looking for pleasure, but they are trying to kill the pain. I stuck my dick in her and she came in like five minutes. She looked at me and said,

"I think you should go now."

I was like, *"What the fuck?"* to myself of course. It was just a surprise to hear her say that after such a dope ass love making session. It was damn near perfect the way we came together and for her to basically tell me to get out of her house was surprising. Later I found out she wanted to make sure I stayed in good standing at home. She, like me, wanted this newfound relationship to continue and wanted me to manage my time and responsibilities effectively and not endanger my status or freedom by doing some dumb shit like staying out later than I had agreed to with my wife.

My dick getting hard again in less than five minutes for round two was my first lesson in the art of allowing and intuiting. You see, I was able to feel her fully; meaning, it was a full body and energetic experience. Up to this point, during sex, I would focus on not ejaculating, or ensuring the woman I was with got an orgasm, or anything other than the numerous subtle feelings happening during the sexual experience. I wasn't thinking about anything except connecting with a beautiful fully built absolute cock diesel woman. And that's what happened. We connected for a full body experience. Every part of the sexual experience felt good. It was a full body experience. Thinking was down to a minimum while experiencing and feeling was at a maximum.

Our lovemaking would be the bomb for months after our first encounter. It stayed perfect until she went on the birth control pill. We weren't using birth control up to that point and I desperately wanted to stay inside of her when I came, but once she went on the pill the quality of our sex life changed. What I found out months later, through research, was the pH of her vagina changed. I started cumming more quickly inside of her and didn't have the same recovery time. It was like my penis was like, "*Yo man, I know you want to stick me back in that pussy, but, I'm telling you that's not the same pussy you're thinking of. It's a lot hotter than it used to be and it's burning me up so I'm gonna cum so I can get out of there.*"

When I was learning about Tantric sex through my teacher Shantam Nityama, he stated the natural defense mechanism for the male penis is to ejaculate when it enters a vagina that is too "hot." Meaning, a vagina at the wrong energetic level (as measured by pH and other factors) can be damaging to a penis. If you look at the penis it's basically a sensitive organ, very fleshy and subject to heat and other elements. It also has its own intelligence, just like every other organ in the body and knows what's good for it and what's not. I know they say, "Don't think with your dick." but you may want to listen to it more often. You wanting to chase some woman is not necessarily your dick thinking. It's you, Holmes.

Needless to say, the inability to connect sexually was part of the downfall of our relationship even though the verbalized reasons were around "time" and "communication," etc. But the essence to me was that our lovemaking connection had changed. I was sad to see her move on, but I have the utmost respect for her and will love her for the rest of my life and she undoubtedly has the best pussy on the planet.

My client Chris came to me in a last ditch effort to save his marriage. We're talking he's down two touchdowns with thirty-seconds left in the fourth quarter and the other team has the ball on his two yard line. That's when I seem to get most of my clients, when things hit DEFCON six in this piece and the President has his hand hovering over the red button. Chris was having trouble feeling sexual passion for his wife and rarely wanted to have intercourse with her. It's not that he didn't love her because he did. That's one of the first tests I perform with couples who come to see me because if the love isn't there then we've got a real problem, but if the love is just buried underneath the plaque that's naturally accumulated during the day-to-day stuff happening in the relationship, then we have a much easier task.

I said, *"Chris, are you attracted to your wife? I mean, has she changed over the years to where you are no longer attracted to her? Has she gained weight?"* He indicated that he was still attracted to her but didn't feel connected to her for some reason, especially during sex. It would be a case where she wanted to have sex and he was praying that one of them would cum so he could watch some television. I guess that's stereotypical in that everyone believes that men are simply looking to bust a nut and then move on to something simple and mundane, like a sandwich and a beer or some video games. But in reality, I know that's not true for men whether they realize it or not.

I knew what was happening with Chris and his wife; there was no deep, energetic connection between them. Meaning, he couldn't really feel her on a deep level and therefore, he wasn't being nourished by her on a soul level. You see, what really draws us to people is the sense that there is a deep spiritual connection between you and them. It's not about the surface stuff like looks or status, but rather the soul connection. My feeling was that Chris fell in love with his wife because of a sense of having this soul-level connection with her, but was never really able to experience that connection in its fullness. The first years of their relationship were spent knowing the jewels were there and being able to almost taste them, but never being able to actualize them. This happens to many people who enter in relationships that later end in separation or divorce. A dream not realized.

I had to teach Chris how to feel on a soul level. It was time to go below the surface.

Me: "*Chris, here's what I need you do to. I need you to understand that you haven't been taught how to feel. For boys growing up in this culture we are usually on one of two extremes, either we shut down the feeling process completely because we are told emotions are for pussies or we open up completely and confuse that with being feminine and believe we are gay. I want us to find the middle ground where you give yourself permission to feel and enjoy sex and when I say feel I mean feeling the subtle aspects of sex like soft touch, her sounds in your ear, feeling every quiver of her body and allowing it to penetrate your soul. You should be able to achieve orgasm, not ejaculation, but orgasm just by sitting still inside of her and breathing. Just sitting inside of a woman without moving and intentionally breathing is an extremely intense experience when you allow the energy to build and stay open to feeling it.*"

Chris: "*Um…yeah.*"

I think Chris understood what I was saying, but didn't really get it. I gave him some simple approaches to dealing with his wife in a more holistic way like starting foreplay during the middle of the day before he got home. Simple stuff like text messages letting her know that he can't wait to see her when he gets home or maintaining physical contact with her when she's in the kitchen or around the house. Next, he was to take his time with her before proceeding to oral sex or intercourse. I wanted him to lay next to her with both of them still wearing something and to run his hand across her curves, skin, and face and get an appreciation for her contours and subtle make up. Notice her responses to his touch and the heat coming from his body, and most importantly stay present with how he is feeling throughout the process. How do you feel when she twitches and responds to your touch? What thoughts enter your mind? Do you feel any emotions that maybe you hadn't allowed yourself to feel? These details are important and will help him on his journey to feeling. Once he had done this preliminary connecting with his wife, he could then move to the more traditional foreplay like kissing her nipples, abdomen, and clitoris. In other words, don't just jump into the pussy headfirst.

Chris was hopeful at the possibilities, but skeptical at the same time. The hope probably came more from the need to do something at this late stage in the marriage. My first feedback from Chris was that he was able to do many of the things I told him, but that his wife seemed to benefit more than him. She enjoyed the text messages and sweet words, the soft touches and the fact that he took his time with her more than in the past. She seemed to be wet and more ready to have sex than usual, but things didn't change much for him. He still felt disconnected from her and the enjoyment level didn't change much.

A few months later, I got a call from Chris saying that he had the most unusual and unexpected experience. He was out of town on business and called his wife on the phone to check in on her and the kids when he suddenly felt very close to her as if she was in the hotel room with him. He could feel her heat and noticed that his heart was racing a bit and that he wanted her very bad. They ended up having phone sex and he had one of the most intense sexual experiences of his life. He came so hard he thought the people in the room next to him were going to call hotel security. It was like a release that was tied to a powerful orgasm then followed by an intense ejaculation. They started fucking like rabbits as soon as he got home a few days later and the physical experience was much more intense than it ever had been. The bottom line is he was able to feel on a deeper more intense level. Instead of sex being an erogenous zone experience where the penis was the primary focus he was able to feel energy in his entire body down to his bones.

Did her pussy change? No! His ability to feel her and feel in general changed. He's experiencing life on a whole new level including sex with his wife.

He said, *"Carl, my wife has the best pussy on the planet."*

CHAPTER 2

IT JUST FEELS GOOD

We can never forget that at our core feeling good is our greatest desire as well as our birthright. As you learn about the higher aspects of your sexuality and spirituality, never forget this simple truth.

IT JUST FEELS GOOD

WHAT FEELS BETTER THAN taking all your clothes off and getting under the covers with the sweetest little thing you could ever lay your eyes on? Damn! Smooth skin against every part of your body: legs, chest, arms, face, hands, inner and outer thighs feeling the softness – just a tender little thing. Even looking into each other's eyes, knowing what's about to pop off, feels good. Her guiding my cock into some wet hot puccienda. Yes mama; guide that motherfucker straight to heaven. Nice! I remember some of the elders like my man Kesabnebu and Dick Gregory talking about sex. They would describe it as this butt naked Garden of Eden experience. I could almost see them in my mind on top of their woman going up and down in an old school fashion. I always saw the old school men as doing more of a humping type of thing during sex – kind of like Holy Roller preacher type sex (that's missionary position, jumping up and down in the pussy type of fucking). I'm not sure why I thought that because they probably fuck the same way we all do, but that's what came to my mind. It was a good vision because I could see myself at age seventy with a rock hard dick still taking care of my business just like these elders.

There's a lot of technical talk about tantra and the healing aspects of sex to the point we sometimes forget the motherfucker just feels good. Don't forget the basics and thus bore the crap out of peoples. Feel me? It feels good. And just feeling good does wonders to the mind, body, and spirit. Feeling good in and of itself is healing. It lifts up our mood, lowers our stress and facilitates the rejuvenation process. Don't fuck with me on this one. So when I say sex is healing this is what we are talking about. Who are we? Me and Marvin of course. Sexual Healing is where it's at. All I'm saying is let's recognize the healing aspect of sex and act appropriately and let's maximize the experience. I mean, if you're going to take time and do something you might as well do it right. Why have an ejaculation when you can have an ejaculation and multiple orgasms? Why help your girl get to one orgasm rather than twenty? Trust me, she'll like you better with the twenty joint.

When I started my journey learning about the metaphysical and alchemical aspects of sex I got really technical and stiff with it and forgot sex felt good. Sex became a chore to say the least. Not only was I not enjoying it, but my wife was like, "What the fuck?!" I would be doing some breathing technique while in the missionary position, making funny inhaling noises while I pulled my gut in and squeezing my butt checks together and my wife would look at me like, "*What's up with the epileptic seizure technique? Should I call a doctor? Please cut all the crap out and start pounding this pussy like it stole your lunch money.*" On the real tip, my wife knew what I was doing, but sex wasn't fun for either of us during our 'learning' years. It became a monotonous chore filled with tension like a thirty-foot birdie putt on the eighteenth hole at a major golf championship to force a playoff.

So no matter what technique or lesson you learn from this book, or anywhere else, remember to keep it light and enjoy yourself first and foremost. I know that's easier said than done sometimes, but it's worth keeping in mind.

IT JUST FEELS GOOD

CHAPTER 3

TO MEET A
TRUE MASTER

*If you ever have the chance to meet a true master, regardless of
the discipline or art, honor them and yourself with your utmost
attention and regard. Forsake not the greatest gift life has to offer
– wisdom in human form.*

TO MEET A TRUE MASTER

FROM ONE PERSPECTIVE, YOU could say I'm from the old school. I don't believe most people who call themselves masters of the esoteric sciences are actually masters. This includes yoga, spirituality, energy healing, martial arts, astrology, tantra, or whatever. Sorry! I don't care if you've been to India fifty times. It doesn't make you a master of yoga or spirituality or tantra for that matter. You could bend over, look directly into your ass crack and do every banda and mudra in the book while chanting mantras until the cows come home. We are in the West and there is such a vacancy of wisdom in the Eastern arts and sciences, you can read a book or two and set up shop, studio, or healing center in no time and make a gang of cash. I got it. And believe me, I'm not trying to break up anybody's hustle. Do your thing. All I'm saying is there are some true initiates out here and we see through all of the B.S. It's not to say there is no benefit to doing the work that's being done or teaching others because there is. Everyone attracts the teacher they are ready for.

I made a major transition in my life in 2005. I moved completely away from the spiritual society that I was affiliated with for ten years. I was mentally and emotionally apart from this group since 2004, but my wife was still heavily affiliated with the group. Not only that, but our family was living with three other families who were deeply affiliated with this group. We had a plan of moving out to land together and living sustainably together. The group broke apart when it came down to dealing with details around finances and governorship. Go figure, right? Money and politics. Oh well. So much for people of a higher consciousness working it out amongst the inferiors and less learned. The whole experience taught me a lot about life and myself. It's always nice when you get a chance to see your own ass.

Once my wife left the group we moved out to the really nice suburbs, first in Downtown Reston, Virginia and then to Alpharetta, Georgia. Nice, and much different from living in Washington, DC. One of the members of the Land Group, Master Yao Inyamate, was and still is a great friend. He invited Kenya and I to be a part of a spiritual retreat he was sponsoring in Virginia. He wanted Kenya to perform ritual services and help the women possess their feminine selves. That's one of the services my wife offers. She possesses source, and specifically she can catch the spirit of a great many entities and communicate their message to all those who dare behold it. The headliner of the retreat was a Tantric Master named Shantam Nityama from California. It was my experience with Nityama that would change me forever. It was through Nityama I would learn to appreciate my gifts of connecting with women.

Have you ever brought a woman to orgasm without touching her? No? Wait, forget orgasm, how about just any level of intense sexual pleasure without physical contact? No again? Well, me either, up until that point. At least, not knowingly, but that was about to change. I never heard of any shit like that. I wasn't even searching for it. I can't say a woman's orgasm was much on my mind, but it was after that weekend. It became my focus.

I remember listening to a lecture from a Tantra Master named Master Sunyata Saraswati, author of *Jewel in the Lotus*. I was on the line with him while he was doing a radio show and a caller asked how the student would know if they had come into contact with a true master. Master Sunyata told the student he would feel his energy and would have an inner knowing he was the teacher for him. He implied his energy could be felt through his voice. Nityama spoke with a calm assuredness. He took his time and allowed his words to sink into everyone's consciousness.

It was the same with his Tantric bodywork. He took a volunteer from the audience. Next thing I know, a woman emerges butt naked from the bathroom – a thick, well-put together female. Nice! This should be good. Actually, after seeing her in all her glory the demonstration was already worth it for me. Very nice! Oh yeah, but the point is, this woman volunteered to lie on the table and be worked on by the master. Now what is he going to do? Did I say she was thick and beautiful? Her body was like Oya on the cock-diesel tip. Breasts were the perfect size and coming at me like a 3-D movie. Skin smooth like a baby's ass; plump juicy lips that all of the men in the room just wanted to suck off of her face and swallow whole. Straight, white teeth and big, beautiful, brown eyes. Oh, yeah, and an ass that looked like two midgets curled up in the fetal position hibernating up in her cheeks. But, with some women it's not just about the individual physical characteristics, but how they all move together. Have you ever been to a soulful symphony? Have you ever seen a soulful symphony? Now close your eyes and see it as the instruments come together in a milky sound eargasm that's smooth as buttermilk on a Sunday morning. She was beautiful; and she was butt ass naked. Nice!

This is another sign you're a master. When the finest, thickest thing in the whole camp gets butt naked on your behalf in front of a bunch of strangers. Do you feel me on that? And this is black people, which is an important factor here. Black folks are super conservative when it comes to their sexuality, bodies, and nakedness. In all my experiences working tantra, I've observed that white women will line up butt naked to volunteer and lay on the table. On the contrary, very few black women are down with it. They've got something on. Which has always been cool with me because the demonstrations are even more effective. People leave the seminar saying, "*Did you see that? She was fully dressed and still had an orgasm and homeboy didn't touch her. God damn!"* If the woman was naked they may think I brushed her clitoris or something and caused the orgasm that way.

So, this beautiful woman laid down on the table. She was a bit shy, but Nityama made her feel comfortable. He covered her with a sheet and spoke to the eager audience. The more I think about it, she wasn't the only one who was nervous. Everyone was, especially the other women in the room. Nervousness and skepticism could definitely be felt from the women. The men were cool. They had already gotten their money's worth seeing a thick-ass dime piece walk through the crowd butt nasty style. Yessiirrr.

Nityama went on to explain how beautiful the female body is. He didn't have to tell me that. It was as plain as the sun is bright. I just saw it first hand. He said the female orgasm was one of the most beautiful sights a man could see and proceeded to give us background on the beauty of the female form. Next he began to shine on her. Shining is when a man focuses his light upon a woman through his body without touching her. He started on her pussy and spent some time moving his hand up and down over her pussy all the while never touching her. Keeping his hands about six inches to a foot over her. Next he proceeded to move his hand up her centerline going from the abdomen, stomach, chest, throat, and over her face. I watched his hand the whole time. It seemed to shake as if affected by her energy in some way or affected by the energy he was projecting though it. As I watched his face I could see his focus and attentiveness to her. He watched her so closely. I'm trying to remember when I've seen a man be that focused on and attentive to a woman, myself included. Oh yeah, I've seen it before. On television shows where they show brain surgeons operating on a patient. It was similar to that, but there was this care, love, and nurturing component with him. It

66

was like he sincerely loved her. This alone taught me a lesson and helped me appreciate my natural energy. I've always been the type to not only love the women I'm with, but honor and cherish their whole being as well.

After about ten minutes I noticed this woman started to move around a bit. It didn't look like organic movement; meaning, she wasn't going with the flow, but kind of resisting something. Yep, she was struggling with something. It was almost like when someone is telling you to relax, but you insist on holding tension in your body. Or maybe, you don't want to do something in public so you hold in your energy. After a while I understood she didn't want to lose her fucking mind in public. She didn't want to jump all over the table, but that's exactly what she ended up doing – straight giving up the Holy Ghost. Laughing, crying, moaning. It became a natural thing where she no longer resisted, but allowed herself to flow. It was like sweet poetry in motion.

What was even more interesting was that after about thirty minutes or so the women in the audience began crying because her form and expression were so beautiful and eloquent. The vulnerability she displayed and the care that Nityama gave to her were an example and reminder of what all women really want from their man in relationships and in every experience for that matter. These were the same women who were initially pessimistic about the process and Nityama's intentions and felt upset that this "skank" would take off all her clothes in front of these barbaric, sex-crazed men, not to mention this old "Tantra Master" who was probably just trying to get a piece. These women were pissed in the beginning. They tried to hold it in, but it was clear. Their faces said, "*What is this old negro going to do with this young beautiful black woman butt naked on the table. Why don't you take your clothes off mister master tantra man? Why don't you lay butt naked on the table mister master bodywork expert? We all know you just want to fuck this youngin'. You just want to get your feel on you horny bastard. This is some of that old bullshit."* Yep. And I'm not exaggerating either.

The demonstration session continued until this woman had repeated orgasms and seen all parts of her past, talked to her ancestors, and played with and hugged the goddess within her own being.

Sometimes you see something so outside of what you've ever seen or could ever imagine you don't know how to react to it when you do see it. That's how most of the room was at the conclusion of the bodywork demonstration. From that point on I made it a point to pay very close attention to everything Nityama said and did. I watched how he carried himself, moved, talked, dressed, and everything. I knew I was in the presence of a master. Everyone else didn't necessarily view it that way. You have to be receptive and ready to receive a master into your life and the fact is most people just aren't there. They are still living inside of their head and ego and have fears of being taken advantage of or being made of mockery of by friends and family. But I didn't have that fear. I was ready to learn.

I would spend more time with Nityama over the coming months and received more insight and training on his Nitvana Bodywork technique and understanding our sexuality as human beings. Some of the things I learned were:

- A woman owns her orgasm and there's no limit to the number of orgasms she can have
- Sex is a woman's act
- A woman's form is one of the most beautiful things on the planet
- Sex begins well before the bedroom

- All women want to be free sexually whether they realize it or not

I am thankful and grateful for the experience for it has changed my life forever.

CHAPTER 4

I CALLED
HER SUNSHINE

The truth is, love is all around us and walks through the door in the very moments we need it most. If we walk with this truth we can receive life's gifts and let them go when their time has passed.

A GREAT LESSON I learned from one of my teachers is that the world is abundant by nature. There's never a need to covet or possess something as "yours" because the universe will always provide what you need. Even in times of controversy and despair a way or resource will always be provided.

♠

When you're a young man you dream of a gorgeous butt naked woman just appearing in your bed one night ready to practice various sexual techniques on you. Like you roll over and there she is naked, talking about if she doesn't get a dick in her mouth soon she just doesn't know what she's going to do with herself. My logical response, "*Oh, wow. I just happen to have some fresh penis right here if you'd like me to help you out of this dire situation.*" That's a young man's dream, but how often does it happen that way? Pretty much never. We have to work for every ounce of sex we get. Pussy dropping from the sky may happen once every seventy years or something during a good karma lifetime.

It's important to note that the law of attraction plays an important part in the whole tantric sex experience. Meaning, you will attract the experience you believe you deserve and/or the experience you are ready to receive.

In the summer of 2008 my wife and I "officially" opened our marriage. What does that mean? It means I could stick my penis in whomever I felt was worthy of some of the cleanest, meanest penis (as Biggie would say) this side of the Mississippi. Yes, we were both free to interact with other people in any way that we saw fit. From one standpoint that seems like a basic human right, but the truth is that right doesn't exist in traditional marriage. The modern day marriage institution and arrangement has a number of ownership overtones and undertones about it to the point you really have to watch your step, else you be considered in violation. To be straightforward, the husband owns his wife's vagina and the wife owns her husband's penis. So the opening of the marriage marked the dissolution of one of the ownership covenants or at least the beginning of that dissolution.

During the summer solstice we had a gathering of the minds at our house. This was mostly a business arrangement, but included an interesting personal aspect as well. You see my wife's love interest Cain had come to town to be a part of the festivities and officially open our marriage up. They had been together already, but I had not met him yet.

The day wore on as individuals made their business presentations to the group. Cain's girlfriend was there as well and made her presentation. She is actually the subject of my next chapter entitled 'The Art of the Subtle Touch'. She was beautiful, confident, but had some issues with Cain dating Kashi, which was perfectly natural. They were in a different place than Kashi and I. We were married for thirteen plus years at the time and expanding out into new territory; whereas, they were still trying to establish their relationship and look toward marriage.

Many dynamics took place throughout the day as people socialized with one another, but they wouldn't all be revealed until later that night and throughout the weekend. Eventually, Cain's girlfriend went back to her hotel room so that he and Kashi could spend time together. As the late evening and night started to settle in people started to pair up in some cases and others decided to head home until tomorrow's meetings. I went to bed after being fairly tired from playing host, doing my own presentation, and performing a number of other duties throughout the day. I was actually looking forward to getting some sleep, but little did I know it wasn't going to be easy. This was actually going to be a difficult night for me.

That night was actually a rough night for me on many levels, but it would be my first official initiation into the laws of tantra. The night was tough because I was dealing with heavy jealousy issues regarding my wife dating another man. Yes, I understood the validity of an open relationship intellectually, but it's a whole different story when that shit is up in your face. So when nighttime rolled around, I got into our bed by myself in the master bedroom. Kashi wanted me to sleep there and said her and her boyfriend would find another spot. Needless to say I couldn't sleep. All I could think about was her fucking this dude Cain.

I can't tell you how hard it is for men transitioning out of a place of jealousy and insecurity, especially when it comes to 'our' women with other men. You might as well just stick our balls in a vice grip and crank that motherfucker until we pass out. Then when we wake up, crank that shit some more. Yeah, that's about how it feels. Like getting tortured in the most sensitive part of your body. Well, that's not far from the truth. A man's mental and emotional being is the most fragile part of his core and if you want to affect him in a deep profound way, you do it mentally. And actually you see women do it all the time. They fuck with men's heads. It's where a woman's power resides – her mental acuity. Women can easily make a man feel like shit or like the king of the planet. It's her talent, role, and gift. So needless to say, I had to battle these thoughts in my head.

But the important lesson for me is that I never knew these types of emotions existed in me. I never considered myself to be a jealous person or having relationships based on ownership. I've never had a girlfriend of mine cheat on me or express an interest in another man before meeting my wife. The closest thing I remember to feeling jealous was over my ex-girlfriend's past love relationships. We were together and in a committed relationship, but I still felt jealous of her earlier boyfriends and I never resolved why I felt that way. It wasn't a major issue for us because these were boyfriends of the past. Nothing was in my face so I never really had to deal with it, but looking back on it, I would have to say they were silly, childish emotions. Today when I coach women I instruct them to turn and run if their love interest wants to know their sexual history. That's some major insecurity right there and I mean major. And just because I didn't deal with it and swept it under the rug doesn't mean its not affecting my current relationships, even the monogamous ones. As a matter of fact, in thinking back about my ex-girlfriend, the jealousy played a part in us breaking up. I really had expected us to be married and she did too. I think everyone who knew us expected that. But my constant thoughts about her with other men got in the way of me being able to bond with her fully and made us splitting apart that much easier. So yes, those jealousy issues had a major impact on my relationships.

These jealousy issues played out with Sunshine later on in our platonic friendship. I remember feeling jealous of an encounter she had with a particular man and it made it hard for me to be close to her. It's a bullshit emotion and it causes many of us to remain children in our relationships. The damage to loved ones and ourselves can be brutal and long lasting.

Let's get back to the night at hand. I didn't realize it at the time but an interesting dynamic was taking shape throughout the day and that night. It's kind of amazing when I think about it. You see, Cain hooked up with another young lady named Sunshine who was there and a mutual friend of ours and there to present to the group. They hooked up that day as well as connecting later that night. Kashi was a great sport about the whole thing and actually ran them a bath and supported them in being comfortable including sticking the two of them in my bed. I guess that move made sense from the fact that every room, couch, chair, blanket, and sleeping bag were taken by the multitude of house guests we had that weekend. So me being in a king size bed by myself I guess you could technically say I had some space. When I look back at these events Kashi really rose to a higher level to accept what happened with Cain and Sunshine and even support them in their experience. In essence her lover came all the way across the country to see her and spend time with her for the first time in over two months, and he had sex with another woman, in her house, which wouldn't be so bad if he could have still performed later that night. I know that may sound crazy, but someone new to open relating would probably spend time wondering if that's within the rules. Like, he came here to see me, but had sex with someone else, is that legal? I guess so, if it's all open.

Ok, so Cain and Sunshine are in my bed kissing or whatever. I'm like is this a college flashback or something. Why am I in a bed with two strangers rolling around necking and shit? That makes sense when you're at the frat house and passed out because you've had too many beers and two of the horniest people at the party find each other and start rolling around the first bed they can find. That actually happened to me at spring break in high school. I was drunk after funneling twelve beers and passed out on the lower bunk when all of a sudden the bed started shaking vigorously. I felt like I was in the belly of a cargo ship and about to puke my guts out, again. Make it stop or rather, can you all please stop fucking four feet above my head. So try to follow me here…Cain and Sunshine are on the bed with me, well, not with me, but in the bed and I'm there too. About twenty minutes later Kashi gets in the bed next to Cain and those two start making out or whatever the fuck you want to call it. I guess she just got tired of getting no action and decided to pull rank. So now you have me, Sunshine, Cain and Kashi in the bed together. So before you start going there in your mind, no, this did not turn into some crazy foursome, although, that may have been pretty dope now that I think about it. But, this really did feel like some college dorm room type of shit. So Cain and Kashi are kissing and shit and Sunshine is laying against my back. My back is turned to the three of these fools the whole time because the last thing I need to do is see this shit taking place. I was able to hold it together well enough when there was no fucking on top of me. But I'm not sure what I would do if a leg drapes over my back or some shit. I might start dragging ninjas down the stairs and into the streets. Or worse yet, if some wet shit lands on my cheek the last bit of mental strength I had may have left me in that moment. But so far so good, relatively speaking. Kashi and Cain are in the mix and Sunshine and I are doing a combination of twirling our thumbs and trying to go to sleep.

Let's stop here for a second. I need to describe Sunshine to you so you can have a full appreciation for what's going on. Sunshine is what I call a pure Lover, meaning, she carries this super sensual energy. She's like a love goddess in so many ways even though she doesn't fully realize it, which makes it that much more attractive. Not so much that she is this sex porn star type, but the purest form of that sensual energy. She's just super nice. She pulls you into her. Like you want to take her home and hide her in the closet and keep her all for yourself. So it was no surprise in the least that Cain got pulled into her that weekend. When I heard about the two of them hooking up I really didn't think twice about it and understood completely. She's just a goddess like that. And it's nothing malicious or targeting either on her part, so no need to go there. It's just a pure attractive energy. What can I say; some women have it like that.

The first time I saw her I wanted to get with her, like, just be with her and around her. Her personality is very pleasant and her smile and laugh will give most men a hardon. I mean she has the most beautiful energy and all you want to do is bask in her glow. On top of all that she was a petite little thing with a great body. So there you have it.

So Sunshine's soft body is on my back and I'm wide awake because Kashi is now in the bed with a negro (okay, okay, Cain) and all I hear is smacking and carrying on behind me. I mean, I don't know what their doing, but it's not fucking. I really don't and don't really want to know, but humans are a curious species aren't we? So after a while I turn around to see what's going on with my own eyes, and to see what's going on with Sunshine since it seems like she got outranked by my wife. As soon as I turn around Sunshine and I lock eyes. So we're looking into each other's eyes and her titties, which felt like two bags of silky cotton covered water balloons were pressed against my chest. Needless to say it was on and popping at that very moment. I kissed her and fell into her energy and her soul. Actually, I dove in and it was sweet. I'm not sure what to say other than Merry Christmas or some other shit because a long lost childhood fantasy got fulfilled. Literally, some beautiful pussy just fell out of the sky into my bed and pressed its titties against me.

I fucked her like a missed her. I fucked her like we were in a long distance relationship and I had been video chatting her for the past ten months, but not allowed to masturbate or anything, just stare at titties. I immediately started eating her pussy, which was some good eating pussy. It was like eating silk. I like it when the pussy is so tight your tongue is like a penis damn near filling up her whole vagina. That was some beautiful pussy. Next I got on her missionary-style and fell every so sweetly straight to the bottom of that tightness and wetness. We made love very gently, passionately, and with the highest regard for one another. She really liked me and I really liked her too. There had always been a mutual attraction there between us and this was like a release of the floodgates.

The other dynamic was the fact that I had been thinking all night about Kashi screwing the negro (okay, okay, Cain). Man! It's amazing how some good loving will heal all of that tension. After Sunshine and I were done I held her in my arms and didn't think any more about Kashi and Cain. My mind was totally at ease. Her and I both needed that interaction that night because her time with Cain was subpar at best; meaning, he didn't take care of the big man business in the way a goddess like that comes to appreciate.

But here is the thing…it's important to understand that we always attract what it is we need in our life. When I work with women I let them know they will attract what they need in a man. Maybe they just need great sex or maybe they want someone who is a great role model for their kids and is willing to take their time and raise her children. Or maybe she just needs a friend that she can talk too. Whatever it is you will attract it to you; especially, after you open up to your feminine nature, which by law is a magnetic and attractive energy. I would like to think I attracted her that night, but it's probably fairer to say she attracted me. Maybe we attracted each other.

I do a bit of Chinese astrology called the Bagua astrology system and in the Bagua system the Lover supports the Visionary. In other words, someone who is born in a Lover year is a natural support for someone born in a Visionary year. Well Sunshine is born in a Lover year which is why she has that Lover energy about her and I am born in a Visionary year. So, she is built to support me in a number of ways, especially, energetically. And you could say I needed support in that moment. I illustrated this in the chart below. Me being a Visionary means I naturally support a Leader.

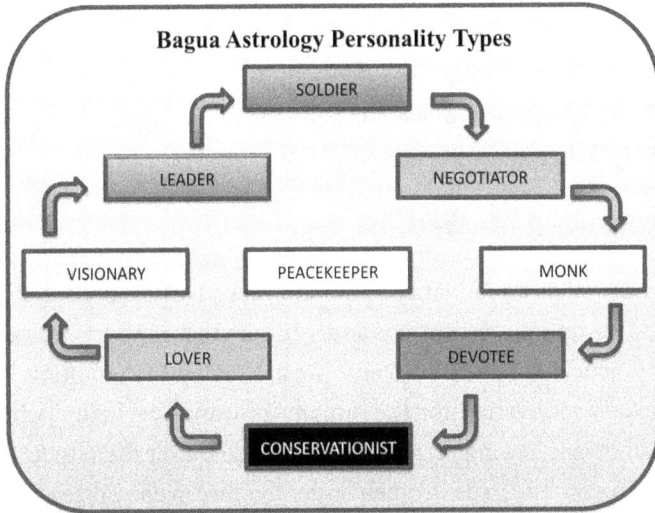

Bagua Astrology Personality Types

	SOLDIER	
LEADER		NEGOTIATOR
VISIONARY	PEACEKEEPER	MONK
LOVER		DEVOTEE
	CONSERVATIONIST	

I can't even remember if I wore a condom or what with Sunshine. It felt like I didn't. It felt like I went raw style and came all up in that there. We made love the next morning too. I fucked her doggy style to the point where Cain and my wife had to leave the room to get some peace of mind. Being with her was my most healing time of my summer. It was the highlight of my summer and year to that point. But most importantly it taught me some of my first tantric laws.

First of all, there is no room for jealousy in a relationship. It's just toxic and I had plenty of jealousy issues. As I mentioned before, I eventually distanced myself from Sunshine a number of years later based on feelings of jealousy and we weren't even relating on any level. It's sad. Second, we will always attract what we need in our life. I know sometimes it doesn't seem that way, but that's probably because we don't recognize the signs or insist on judging the package the blessing comes in.

Jealousy is a Mother

How do we as an "advanced" human race justify jealousy? Why would we uphold institutions and a culture that supports jealousy as a practice? Maybe it's because we are saying that emotion is a necessary motivation for the human. I mean, how many people use emotions like anger, jealousy, or fear to power them to financial success? The issue is much larger than we even realize or care to admit. I remember watching these movies when I was growing up and the evil villain was basically this jealous motherfucker. His brother or friend got more pussy than him and now he's a serial killer ripping women's ovaries out. Or, on soap operas, women would be portrayed as jealous of each other because she had *the* man that everyone wanted or was rich or whatever. I remember watching hours of this crap. But it's not just television. How about when we are children and Timmy has the red toy and the red toy is better than the gray one so now I don't like Timmy anymore? What does Timmy have to do with it? I understand you want the red toy, but to hate Timmy because of it is a bit extreme. I think we see the same thing with class warfare in this country; poor people hating rich and vice versa all because someone has something you don't. Rich people have money and poor people have time. Where did this begin? I guess with the haves and the have-nots.

Webster's online Dictionary defines jealous as "*hostile toward a rival or one believed to enjoy an advantage.*" From my standpoint "advantage" means having something that someone else doesn't, like more money. It doesn't mean that the advantage will be used against you in some aggressive way, right? They just have something that you don't and you don't like that so you're going be aggressive towards them, just because. Another definition says "*vigilant in guarding a possession,*" or as I interpret it, greedy. I mean, what's the purpose of vigilantly guarding something you own? Is it under attack or is there an angry mob waiting to take it from you? We're not talking about locking the car down before you head into the movie theater. We're talking about an "all hands on deck," let's do what we can to protect the prize, type of attitude here. But here's my thing, what are you protecting? Something you own or just your feelings? How do you justify being jealous of another man or woman because your wife or husband looked at them? WTF? You're not protecting her. She actually enjoys the reciprocal attention; trust me on that one, Holmes. Unless the guy jumps over the guardrail and tries to kidnap her, you don't have much ground to stand on here. What you're vigilantly protecting is an idea that you carry in your mind that says your value and worth as a human are dependent on someone doing something in particular to you or for you. Like not showing interest and affection toward another human being. See how fragile we are?

We Always Attract What We Need

In my mind it was safe to assume that my connection with Sunshine was of the utmost benefit to me, at least in that moment. It wasn't just about getting pussy during a tense moment because the truth is, as I said before, I really liked her a lot. She once told me that she could be a soft place to land if I ever needed one. That was the role she saw herself playing in my life. When I look back at it, I guess I had always been that for her in a number of ways when I would give her advice on various things happening in her life.

The biggest challenge I've faced when coaching men and women is their beliefs that they won't be able to find the ONE to be with for the rest of their lives. Everyone is looking for that soulmate or soul connection with someone that will make them feel brand new again. There's nothing like love to make you feel like a million bucks.

One of my clients was newly in an open marriage with his wife. An open marriage means that you can relate to anyone you'd like, even though you're married. His biggest question to me was how do I meet a woman who will accept my open marriage status and also be into me? He said he had met a lot of women, but none of them seemed to be that deep connection and the ones that were close didn't want to date him because he was in an open marriage. It's funny because the fact that he was married wasn't the problem, but the fact that he was open with his wife about what he did seemed to be a roadblock for a lot of women. I guess I can kind of get that because people prefer either the thrill of being on the low with their relationships or having someone all to themselves.

Plus, having another woman in the picture openly sharing a man could be risky because most women don't think they are going to get along with other women. I get it. If there's one thing we haven't been taught to do it's share pussy or penis let alone anything else come to think of it.

Tim: "*Rakhem, I just can't figure out how to approach these women. I will meet with them, we're talking and everything and then I tell them I'm in an open marriage and that's the last I hear from them. It's like it's some kind of turn off or something. On the real, I think I might just stash the wedding ring and not tell any of these women I'm married because I know that's a slam-dunk. I mean everything is going well until they find out about the open marriage thing. It's crazy. I would have thought that by me being honest with them they would appreciate that more than doing the whole down low thing, but that hasn't been the case. What do you think I should do?*"

Me: "*What you're experiencing with these women is common actually so you shouldn't be surprised, but the issue is with you. You have to ask yourself how you feel about your open marriage status and see if you're really being authentic with these women. What I mean is, you should only be attracting women who are on the same wavelength as you. If you're open and proud of it and not hiding it in any area of your life then you will attract women who will appreciate that. However, if you are not being authentic or if you are somehow ashamed of how you are relating then you will attract women who are also ashamed of their actions. Make sense? You have to feel good about being you and I can't tell you where you're not showing up as the real Tim, but it's somewhere, believe me.*"

Tim: "*Ok, so this is the whole mirror concept you talk about where we basically attract our compliments, right?*"

Me: "*Yes. The other side of it is that you need to subscribe to the idea that women will choose you. Don't feel like you need to chase women and don't only go for the women you have always been attracted too. What you should realize is that women will be drawn to you and make their intentions known in some way. These are usually the best women for you to talk to and will be in alignment with who you are and your lifestyle. Make sense?*"

Tim: "*So, don't pursue the women I'm attracted too? I'm not sure on that one. I can't be talking to no ugly females man.*"

Me: "*I feel you, but you're not going to attract ugly women, but maybe some women who you weren't drawn to historically. The best thing about this arrangement is that they will accept you for who you are and at the same time be very supportive of you. Trust me, it's the only way to go and the best way to avoid headache and disappointment. My wife calls the concept 'Womb Choice' where a woman will 'feel' that you are the right one for her even if she doesn't know why.*"

Tim: "*I'm not sure about this one, but I'll give it a try.*"

This is a tough concept for men grasp because we've been conditioned to aggressively pursue the things we want in life, especially women. We're so used to giving chase to women and so used to being rejected that it's just accepted and expected. Not only that, but men have this accumulation of semen in our nut sacks that sends us into a frenzy trying to find a soft nice place to release into with the expeditious quickness. Actually, it gets painful not having sex and masturbation isn't a substitute for pussy. So, being in this fix, is a, well, fix.

I used my experience with Sunshine as a foundation for how I would deal with women going forward. I just switched my mind-set and knew I would always be taken care of and never alone and always loved and nurtured. The more I was able to do this the more it worked. I attracted many women to me who let me know in their own way that they wanted me to talk to them. It is true that many of the women I attracted were not my typical choice of woman. They weren't that "Rakhem Seku Standard" that I had grown to love, but I realized that by talking to these other women outside of my comfort zone, I received something new that I hadn't gotten before. I was treated in ways that I had never been treated and it became even more clear and apparent why it was always best to be chosen as opposed to being the pursuer all the time.

Tim eventually did find the perfect women for him. She was open to his open marriage and supportive of the union him and his wife shared. I was glad we were able to keep the wedding ring on his finger and that he stuck to his guns in telling the truth about his situation. I'm glad he believed that he could find the one to support him and love him and that he learned to be more comfortable and accepting of his openness. I actually knew this woman because she was in our shared circle of friends and followers and interesting enough her nickname was Sunshyne. All is well.

CHAPTER 5

THE ART OF SUBTLE TOUCH

The most powerful sexual experience I've had involved no sexual penetration, no oral sex or stimulation or touching of sensitive parts of the body, no kissing, and no nudity.

ONE OF THE GREAT lessons I learned from my Tantric teachers was the importance and power of subtlety. Through their teaching I observed how subtle and light their actions and movements were, but also the powerful effect they had on people around them. I observed that being slight in word caused everyone to listen more intently, that being reserved in movement caused everyone to respect your space, and that subtleness of touch could cause a powerful ripple effect that could send a women into an orgasmic state for hours. Observing these things from teachers is one thing, but having the experience yourself is something else entirely.

♠

I met Mayling under the strangest of circumstances. She was a girlfriend or something of one of Kashi's boyfriends. Long story that only makes sense if you're in an open relationship, which I am. Yeah, boy! Before I met Mayling my subtle touch experiences were shallow and limited at best. Oh, what is subtle touch? Good question. For me it's a tantric technique that emphasizes that very little is needed to bring about profound and intense pleasure during lovemaking and intimacy. In other words, the less is more rule. The softest kiss. The most gentle touch on the navel, inner thighs, and back can send you into a fucking tailspin.

The idea around subtle touch is that by focusing on each other's energy, as opposed to the physical body, we can affect our partners on the deepest and most profound level. Why? We are essentially, energetic beings and not just physical.

I was intensely attracted to Mayling the first time I saw her because of the intelligence and confidence she exuded. There's something about a woman who is confident because of her look and her intellect and Mayling was that. She also had this smooth chocolate skin complexion in a thin tight package with the perfect amount of muscle tone in the arms and legs, beautiful finger and toe paint (which I have a weakness for), and for a bonus the tightest ass east of Vegas. Not only that but she spoke with eloquence and precision that catapulted her into a higher social class than the rest of us lay folk. She is the kind of woman that is considered a great catch from a man's standpoint. She just had her shit together on so many levels, but had this delicate innocence about her plus the physical tools to match. Plus, for extra bonus points and a shot behind door number three, she had her money situation together and all of that added up gave her this confident swagger with the right amount of cuteness that just turned heads everywhere: the mall, Michigan Avenue, the event seminar, the restaurant. You name it.

So as you can see, I thought highly of this sister (and still do to this day).

Kashi had gone out of town to the lovely island of Jamaica *mon* with one of her community mothers. This was an elder that always looked after our family, especially when we were heavily involved in spiritual culture. She's like that mother away from home. Kind, concerned, resourceful, and strict as nails when she wants to be. She paid for Kashi to go to a raw food retreat for about four days, so it was just me and the children at home.

Mayling calls me and says she was thinking of coming to see me for the weekend. You know, maybe through some clothes in a bag, head to the airport, buy a ticket and check you out for a few days. I told you that having your own money thing is a nice piece. The answer was of course an emphatic "Yes!" See that? I told you in the previous chapter that the Universe always provides what you need, right?

Now here is the thing. I am a gentle man by nature. I'm attentive to women and very present with them during lovemaking. That's just how I've always been. I'm also interested in every single word you have to say; otherwise, I wouldn't be spending time with you. This is sincere all the way around. That's just how I'm wound. I say all of that because my interest is not the big score when it comes to women. I could give a damn about intercourse and women figure that out pretty quickly. Even when they throw a piece of false bait out there to see if I bite, I just don't. Why? I'm not interested in getting into your pants. I'm interested in connecting with you on whatever level that may be. It just means more, feels better, and it lasts longer. I still have a solid relationship with most of the women I have dated because it's always been about our connection and something deeper than personal gratification. Even women where it has been a one or two night stand still feel very connected to me and I do to them.

With Mayling that's how we got to the subtle touch place in our relating. It's exactly what we both needed and defined the purpose of our relationship to the "T." We finally connected on Friday night around eight or so. We shared a simple embrace, not too intimate. The initial hug was a bit on the dry side, but sincere and heartfelt. I could really tell she appreciated being with me, seeing me.

I don't know what we did after that, but we did end up going to bed fairly early. We slept on an air mattress in my room. It was comfy enough. She showered and emerged with the standard t-shirt and panties. Perfectly shaped legs putting me into a slight trance. I showered and had the standard baggy shorts and t-shirt. We laid down together under the covers. Have you ever slept on an air mattress with someone? It can be tricky and a bit of a balancing act. We managed quite nicely though.

She laid on her back and I laid on my side with my right leg over hers. I used my elbow to prop myself up so that my right hand was free. We both wanted to be closer and to feel each other's energy. We were still fully dressed in our nighttime gear. I touched her on the stomach and brought my lips within an inch of her right ear and began slowly inhaling the air from her ear. This is powerful as it feels like I am drawing your very essence up your spine and through your ear. I moved my hand to her left side to feel her softness and squeezed her body very gently. That drew her left leg up and it draped over my right leg. Now we were facing each other. I hovered my lips just above hers without touching and stayed there for a moment. At the same time I was being hypnotized by the warmth and smoothness of her left leg on mine. She moved it ever-so-slightly to the rhythm we were both making. I didn't want her to stop or change anything. The coolness of her feet against my calf completed the paralysis and held me in position from the waist down. It was as if there were three parts of our bodies making love all in unison. Our legs were intertwined, my stomach was gently kissing hers while I controlled the tempo with my hands on her center, and our faces danced and played. I moved my hand to her back and started my breathing technique. I closed my eyes and took a deep breath in, pushing my stomach deeper into hers and ever so slightly pushing my thigh against her pussy. With that inhale I transferred my heat energy into her back and spine. Her back seemed to give way and make a "C" shape with a beautiful arching motion. I exhaled and sent a more intense surge of energy into her. She was pleased and so was I. I moved my lips over her left ear after turning her head into my chest and began to retrieve the energy I just gave to her through my hands. I inhaled and she attempted to ease the feeling by bringing her shoulder up to brace herself. Up to that point her hands were not in play, but just then she touched me on my chest, which increased my energy.

I pulled her body into mine so that we were both on our sides and facing each other. This time I didn't allow any space between us. My chest was against her perfectly shaped breasts. Her leg was draped over mine. I hugged her in an intense embrace while burying her face in my neck and mine in hers. My penis was rock hard, but not intruding into her space. We stayed in that passionate holding and hugging position for what seemed like hours, but was only minutes. Our bodies continued to convulse together as we shared our warmth, passion, and appreciation for each other, as we shared our love for each other.

I continued to touch her very softly on various points throughout her face, neck, back, side, and chest. I also held my hand and lips over parts of her body without touching her at all and she responded in the same way, moving as if to adjust for each new position and transference of energy.

Her face was so beautiful. Watching her eyes roll to the top of her head and hearing her open mouth exhales was like watching an ancient sensual dance. It was feminine essence in its rawest form, like art. Every arch of her back was pleasing to me.

We never kissed. We kept our clothes on the entire night. I never massaged her clitoris and she never touched my penis. We literally bathed in each other's energy for hours. At the end of our sharing I was exhausted; we both were. We both slept well that night.

I was so satisfied with our intimacy I just can't tell you. I didn't want anything more, no head, no intercourse, no wet kiss, nothing. I was totally fulfilled and didn't have the energy to do anything else, but hold her in my arms and go to sleep. You have to understand that a woman with a body and skin tone like hers lying next to me would normally make me want to do the breath stroke in that pussy. I'm talking a total dime here. Our lovemaking was so powerful that I still think of her to this day. She was sweet.

We spent the remainder of the weekend together and everything just flowed. We stayed in touch every once in a while. She called me a few years later and said things were going really well for her on every level and as she was walking in the park and thinking of who to share the moment with, she thought of me.

THE ART OF SUBTLE TOUCH

CHAPTER 6

THE
TANTRIC GODDESS

Some women fully embrace their sexuality and are on a quest to become the essence of Goddessness and it is to those women that all men are forced to be in service to.

THE TANTRIC GODDESS

THE TRUTH IS THAT women and men have a certain degree of control over one another to the point where we subject that person's will to our own. I guess you can say it's a kind of mind control and it's not a bad thing either; especially, when you are with those you love and trust. There are definitely times in our lives when it's good to control others or be controlled.

What men need to understand is that women can control us with their minds, will, and spirit. In many ways women own the minds of men. Sorry about that fellas. This is true especially sexually as they have the ability to dictate your every move. The encounter I described in the Preface of this book was with the woman I call the Tantric Goddess and it demonstrated an aspect of the mind control I am referring to.

♠

There are some women that you see throughout your life that strike you as being so unique and outside of the standard lanes of society that you wonder what it would be like to talk with them or better yet date them. I guess people may have this feeling with celebrities, but I've had it with certain women that just stand out in a special way. It could be the way they carry themselves or the way they dress or speak, but whatever it is it feels like something beyond what you'll ever experience. What I'm saying is most of these women I never even get to talk to.

I had the distinct pleasure of being in a relationship with a woman who opened a gateway to my entire tantric experience. Oh, yeah, tantra, for those who may not know, is an ancient science designed to improve our sexual and intimate experiences.

The study of it will help you appreciate the subtleness of sex and deepen the experience dramatically.

When I first saw her at our Organic Bliss event, I knew I would be seeing her more up close and personal, or at least, I wanted to.

Female Vulnerability; Who's Really In Control?

Tantra is not just touching someone's body softly or staring into their eyes. It's also power fucking. It has it's place just like everything else the only difference is we try to balance it out with the other aspects of sex.

To this day I still don't know how to accurately describe my Tantric Goddess. Beautiful brown skin, voluptuous curves all over her body, the thickest lips on the East Coast, eyes that melt your soul, thick hair primed for grabbing, breasts poking out at you like a 3-D movie, all accentuated with the cutest feet and hands – just nice. I called her the Tantric Goddess because she truly respected the art of tantra. She was into it and responded well to the subtle energies. We could do the soft tantric techniques for hours before having traditional sex and it was nice. But the sex was nice too, and she was captivating. Whenever we would come together for intercourse she would give herself to me completely, but at the same time she would pull me into her with her eyes and her sounds. It made me want to relinquish control of my physical body and hand those controls over to her and that's just what I did whenever we came together. She would hypnotize me with her eyes and pull me into her.

"Pound me Rakhem! Take this pussy for all it's worth. Uncover my treasures. Take me where I have never been and then take me beyond that."

I was under her power. She was mind controlling me and telling me to fuck her without pause and with a relentless abandon. She did it with her vulnerability. She told me with her eyes that I was the one, her warrior, her lover, soldier, and leader. I can't let her down. I have to do this for her. I have to allow her to feel my power. To be rewarded for her submission and loyalty. She deserves everything I have and then some.

And that's what I did. In the missionary position I am able to get the maximum leverage during sex. It puts me in the driver's seat for real. I'm looking down on her and without saying a word letting her know I'm in control of this here ship; even though she has assumed control in this case, but she still allows me to feel like the leader. She needs me to know that I am the leader. She fills me with confidence.

"It's you Rakhem. You are he, him. Don't you see? I do. I feel your power welling inside of me and I honor that.

Take me. Take me now."

My arms in the locked position holding up two beautiful legs upright leaving her soft feet and toes dangling next to my ears, just inside of my side vision of view. My hands and fingers were full of sheets and even some of the mattress. The stress and power I feel in this moment makes me want to put my hands through the mattress and box spring and grab a handful of the wood floor under her bed. My legs are open and knees slightly bent to act as a natural prop and support for my back to give me more power for every thrust. My toes were dug into the mattress and acted as anchors to prevent sliding down the smooth sheets. My head was locked into position about two feet above hers and our eyes were at equal levels. They had to be in order for her to steer and control me. Her eyes looked so innocent and receptive. They pulled me in and spoke to me. They made me love her.

"Do it now Rakhem!"

And I did. With a steady in and out motion I began to fuck her in the dead center of her pussy. Right down the middle. Forget hitting walls for that was a distraction and provided unnecessary friction. Plus, there's no need to focus on hitting walls when your cock is big enough to touch every part of her vagina at the same time. That said, I needed my penis to penetrate her soul without obstruction and with a rhythmic smoothness, precision, and consistency that would send her into a trance and take her out of her conscious mind. Remove all thoughts and ability to think. The earth can be such a boring place.

"Take me to space Rakhem! Take us away together."

As I thrust in and out of her with precise rhythm my body settled into its position. My hands dug deeper into the mattress as my fingers gripped tighter to the sheets and thick mattress fabric to ensure my position. My toes and knees dug deeper into the mattress. I flexed the muscles in my arms and sent a message to her legs that there was no hope of touching the sheets ever again let alone the ground. She continued to steer me with her eyes and I continued to give her all the control I was aware I had. I looked to my right and witness her left foot fluttering helplessly to the rhythm of my movements and it strengthened me. It turned me on even more and hardened my penis beyond what felt like the limits of my skin. I looked to my left and saw here right foot dangling in the same manner, again making my dick even harder than I thought possible. Her ankle bracelet was dancing in rhythm to our music, staying loyal to her ankles and feet. Then I looked back to her eyes to receive more instruction and inspiration. I needed her guidance. I needed to see her beautiful face in its vulnerable position showing me that she was in my hands.

"Rakhem, this is what I needed from you. This tells me you love me. Teach my body to give me pleasure. Show my body it's my servant of pleasure. Pound her into submission Rakhem. I feel you and I love you."

I knew what I had to do. Although she was in control of my body and mind, I was in full recognition of what needed to be done to free us both. It required intense thrusting without any break in rhythm for an extended period of time, for eternity. It would test my internal Leader's consistency. It would test my internal Soldier's willingness to go beyond pain and sacrifice the self to achieve a higher purpose. My Soldier would ignore the fact that my fingers were locking up and that the sweat was running into my eyes blinding me, stinging me. My Soldier instructed my brain to ignore the fact that my knees began to burn and that my lower back began to feel strain and pressure. It also told me to not be pulled in too deeply by her beauty and femininity as I looked into her eyes.

You see, in order for a woman to significantly alter her consciousness during sex a man must replace her normal sensations with rhythmic sound and vibration. Meaning, most women don't go into trance or go into a heightened orgasmic state because they are too aware of their physical surroundings. It's like a female deer trying to eat grass in the woods, but continues to hear rustling in the bushes. She can't enjoy her food; she can't relax. Through the rhythmic motion of my thrusts she lost sensation in the rest of her body and when you lose sensation in your body, your mind begins to look for other things to sense and experience and for women that means by nature they will search within. Why? There's nowhere else to go. The physical world is off limits and inaccessible because you no longer have the ability to perceive it. As the man taking her to this place, I could see her going within, gradually making the transition from extroverted thinking woman to introverted surrendered goddess.

That's actually the height of the sexual experience for me. Watching a woman transform into her highest self through total relaxation and surrender. That's what tells me I'm impacting her life in a profound way in this very moment. That she feels protected and secured by my Soldier and knows my Leader is present because every time she comes back to the physical plane she sees my eyes locked in on hers with intensity and care. So much so, it allows her to drift back into the inner planes and talk the angels and the ancestors once more.

I saw it in her. As time continued her normal sensory preceptors began to fade, as all she could feel was my steadiness. She began to dismiss the thoughts in her mind that told her I was going to stop or cease and a new set of beliefs began to take hold telling her she could let go of everything because Rakhem has got me. I can ride his energy to a new space-time reality and to a deeper feeling of my self. I can discover my inner goddesses who lie deep beneath my daily waking experience on earth. I can meet them, hug them, talk with them and invite them to be a part of my life from henceforth. And so it was.

I continued to thrust inside of her steadily until I almost couldn't feel myself. Until the reality around me started to fade just a bit and I found myself less concerned with time or space. Her sounds and cries of passion became background noise. The room got darker and I could hear my breathing from the inside of my body. Somewhere in these moments of passion, pleasure, and purpose we enter a trance state that allows us to continue our journeys with steadiness and resolve. I was there and it was peaceful and good and forever. Once I transcended the illusions of time, pain, and selfishness I was able to relax into a place between our world and hers while maintaining enough awareness to stay present with her throughout our journey.

At the end of that experience I would have thought I would be exhausted and physically incapable of anything other than sleep, but that wasn't the case and I knew why. The only way to maintain both stamina and rhythm for that length of time is by altering my own mind. By going into a state of trance and possessing the Leader and Soldier talents within me. This is more than being in shape, which is a prerequisite. It's about tapping into a part of you that desires to do what's required at any cost and for her. This experience wasn't just about her and for her. It was about us and my ability to go beyond myself was put to the test.

We never completely finished our work together. We made love many times, but both of our transcendental sessions were cut short by external circumstances. Maybe we created those interruptions through out subconscious minds because we just weren't ready to see what was on the other side and uncover all of her treasures. But the work doesn't have to be completed by me. Now that she has the desire and expectation she can attract the experience to take her all the way home.

Warning to Men, Advisory to Women

I remember my time with Tantric Goddess being exhausting to a degree. There were two reasons for this: #1) I believe the mental aspect of our relationship took a heavy toll on me and #2) I didn't know how to manage my own energy and will in this relationship. With power comes responsibility. If you are going to move a person towards a particular end then you must also energize and nourish them for the accomplishment of that task. In other words, *if you are giving me what I want then I must give you what you need if I desire it to continue.* It's a metaphysical reality to relating to someone and if violated makes people feel unappreciated, tired, or used. Some of this was happening in our relationship where the nourishment was lacking. But on the other side being controlled feels good and has a tremendous up side and you can't get caught up in subjecting yourself to that feeling and position all the time no matter how good it feels. I know I was caught up in feeling and the bottom line is I was exhausted.

THE TANTRIC GODDESS

CHAPTER 7

THE POWER OF STILLNESS

I learned that the greatest feeling and pleasure during sex is in the feeling discovered inside of the subtlest of movements and the quietest stillness I could create with my partner.

ONE OF MY OTHER great tantric lessons was learning the power of stillness. Throughout my life I had been conditioned to fuck like I was trying to start a fire with two sticks. Master Sunyata Saraswati called it "friction" sex or "barbaric sex." You've got to give it to the old school masters. They just come with the hardcore frankness that's rare these days. I remember when Master Sunyata was doing a radio show and a young lady called in and said she had been practicing yoga. When Sunyata asked her what kind she said Bikram (Hot Yoga). Sunyata said, "That's not yoga dear; that's stretching." – too funny. What can you say to guy with fifty plus years of practicing experience in Tantra, Tai Chi, and Chi Gong? How about, "Yes sir."

♠

Queen and I hit it off immediately. Our energy is very similar; meaning, we are both laid back in general, but very intense when it comes to sex and relating; both good communicators.

Sex between us was intense and free. I love that. Pulling out is for suckers. We had sex the first night we met up. Nothing beats that back seat love. Head and wet pussy with traffic whizzing by on one of the busiest streets in Manhattan. Rain falling just enough to make the back seat even more comfortable and desirable. The nighttime darkness supplying the perfect blanket like a Romulan cloaking device. There's something about making love in public; watching people walk by. Being close enough to touch a taxi. Wondering who is looking for a good enough time to check a car and see a free freak show. No one. Nice! Then there's the fleeting thought of a cop tapping on the window with a flashlight, asking us to step out of the car. I wonder how that conversation would go?

Cop: "*What were you kids doing there in the back seat?*"

Me: *I'm thinking why would he ask me the question? Does he need an official guilty plea or will him seeing my cock in homegirl's mouth suffice for evidence? Dude, just book me.* "Um, I was helping this young lady find her contacts. I think one of them fell on the floor in the back seat so we both got back here to look for them."

Cop: "*Huh. Is that so? How exactly did her ass cheeks get pressed against the back window? Wait, let me guess. She lost her panties too, right?*"

Me: "*No she didn't lose her panties. That's the craziest thing I've ever heard. We thought the contact lens might have gotten stuck on her clothes so I had her take them off so we could shake them loose. Then we thought the contact fell on my pants and I noticed that my zipper was partially open so I opened it all the way to see if the contact fell on my cock. It was hard to see so she said she would try to feel the contact with her tongue. And that's how my cock got down her throat. My hand was gripping the back of her head because I wanted to help guide her so she didn't eat the contact by mistake.*"

Cop: "*Any drugs in the car? Meth? Acid? Shrooms? Ecstacy? How about you pull your cock out of her mouth and put it back in your boxers and step out of the car Mr. Smart Guy. Mr. Funny Man. You know, they love cocks in the downtown precinct too, except based on the roughneck guys I've seen down there, you may be the one tasting for contact lenses. Not in the mood for jokes anymore, are we Mr. Funny Man?*"

The New York streets are actually kind of boring and pre-dictable. Not much action usually so no one looks for it. I could probably walk through Central Park with florescent orange bikini shorts on and no one would notice. Fuck a hotel room. Where's the excitement in that? Nothing like those city streets.

There were two experiences that Queen gave me during our unfortunately brief relationship. The first was how this woman gave me head. It was always slow, focused, and intense. She was so attentive to my cock throughout the process. It was like a science project to her or something. Actually, now that I think about it, it was like she was feeling for contact lenses. She would study the cock, then proceed with a precision-style fellatio offering; then stop again and intensely study the cock for results, changes, or impacts. I could feel her listening to my moans and sound effects, studying my body movements, listening to the gods instruct her on how to proceed next. She wasn't even there. She gave herself to the process; possessed the goddess of bomb ass top piece. She would put me in her mouth again and just hold me there. No movement. Like she was taking her own temperature and my tool was the thermometer. And that was the thing. The stillness of just holding my cock in her mouth along with the care she was giving me was otherworldly. Not moving, not humming, not looking in my eyes, but just meditating on my shit. It's what brings the emotion out of me not just the semen. I wanted to cry, yell, ex-press something loud and uncontrolled. You see in all my years of fucking, I've never had an experience that in and of itself brought out the emotion that was locked into the core of my being. Sure, I've been emotional and had sex with my girlfriend on some old break-up-to-make-up-type stuff or hooked up with a sister that I hadn't seen in forever, but had been torturing myself with phone conversations and picture-looking for months prior to seeing her.

Yeah, that's some emotional and exciting pussy. But, what about a woman that loves you so strong and so intensely that she brings out what you never knew was there. She brings out that part of you that wants to cry and release all the bullshit you've been holding onto since youth. All that stuff that you thought you shrugged off and said didn't affect you in the least bit. Like those conflicts I had in grade school.

Friend: "*Don't listen to that fool, Rakhem.*"

Rakhem: "*Yeah, I'm not. He's a punk ass anyway and he better hope I don't see his ass again.*"

But, I did listen to what he said. Those words (fill in the blank for your own life) did impact me. I believed them even though I didn't want too. I knew they were true. I knew he had identified a part of me that was weak or wasn't strong. But tell me, where and when and how do I release that because it's already too late. I've internalized those words and they've become a part of my DNA, my core. Someone needs to convince me of something different, otherwise I'll carry that for life. These things will haunt me in my subconscious being and get in the way of my relationships, confidence, money, you name it.

She released it. And I felt safe enough in her presence to let it go. Well a portion of it anyway. It was that kind of head, that kind of sex, and that kind of lovemaking. Feel me now? Most men have this hardcore exterior when they make love or have sex with women. No vulnerability. Not even admitting that you love this woman when you do. That's so hilarious to me. That she is important to you and counts for so much. I know you do even though you call her demeaning names or tell your boys she doesn't mean anything to you. I see you, Holmes.

I told her that too. I said, "*You meditate on my penis. It's like your going into Samadhi with it or something.*" She said, "*Yes, I like to take my time.*"

When she held me in her mouth what I noticed was a gradual increase of energy in my penis and nut sack. It just got more and more intense. Now there are two ways to look at this: (1) that there was an actual gradual increase in energy between her and I that was building up in my cock or (2) that the energy was already there, but because I was used to friction sex I had not been sensitive to the energy or aware of it. It was probably a combination of both. I know with friction sex you miss many of the subtleties taking place. It's actually harder to feel during friction sex. For me, the harder and faster I go the less I can feel and the less likely I will ejaculate. But the slower I go and the more I take my time, the more I can feel. The more intense the experience is for me. It can be so intense that's it's hard to be in that moment and just hold it without resisting the desire to move. It's like exercise. The easiest exercises always involve movement while the most difficult involve stillness or very slow motion. Ever notice that? Try just standing in the squat position with your knees bent for ten minutes versus doing up and down squats. I'll take the up and down squats for $300 and a shot at a thirty-minute break.

The stillness not only included her mouth around my cock, but also her hands. Her right hand held a position at the base of my penis. I remember looking down and seeing her four fingers wrapped around my penis while her mouth completely enveloped the head and upper shaft of my penis. Her hands were actually slightly warm, but they felt cool on my penis probably because of the moisture she had built up in her palms.

Every time she did that, I ejaculated; every single time. And I don't usually ejaculate from head because it's rarely intense enough. As a matter of fact, with most women, I need to focus on ejaculating in order to do it from head — as in, think about other shit. Not all women, but most. And that's the thing… giving proper head is a specialty. Think about it. You're not engaging any other part of my body, only my dick and my mind. That's it. So to get me to ejaculate with head you need to get the intensity popping off something fierce through the penis and get into my head (pun intended). And that's just what Queen did. She intensified the energy, which is perfect for me because I connect with women based upon their energy and not based on physical attraction. Friction sex has little-to-no appeal to me, especially after having experiences like this with Queen.

My ability to connect with a woman in this way is usually dependent on our energetic connection or in other words, my ability to feel her from a distance. If I can feel your energy, I don't need to touch you at all let alone bang you. Not only that, but when I have an energetic connection with someone I can feel them on the inside. It's like a heart connection as opposed to a surface or superficial connection. Queen and I had an energetic connection and that made our physical interactions even more intense. It's one reason why she could touch me in the slightest way and I feel it so intensely.

The key is to allow yourself as a man to feel in this way – to allow yourself to feel your lover's energy without touch. If you can do it, the intimacy and lovemaking will be seamless and intense.

THE POWER OF STILLNESS

CHAPTER 8

A LOVE SUPREME
My Relationship with Love

When you're in love, there's a thin line between happiness and hurt.

ONE THING I LEARNED is that being "in love" is giving yourself permission to feel every emotion you can possibly feel, the good, the bad, and the excruciatingly painful. But what I also learned is that if you don't allow yourself to actually feel and experience fully in your life and relationships, then love will ultimately come up and bite you on the ass.

♠

There was a period of my life, while I was in New York City that I went through an intense depression. You know it's depression because you can hardly move. It's like the weight fairy comes and laces your entire body with intricately-woven body weights. Then the weight fairy goes into your brain and puts a series of weights on it making it feel like it's sinking into itself so that even lifting your head off the pillow is like climbing Mt. Everest. You don't shower. You wear the same clothes and underwear for days straight. Shaving suddenly becomes optional. You don't care about people's opinions of you. Depression is really harder on the people around you. Personally, I like being depressed. I don't try to be depressed because I don't get much done, but it's a cool state to be in; especially, if you don't panic while you're in it. You just let it run its course and before you know it you'll feel right as rain. The only problem is the rest of the world is expecting you to function at a high level, but being depressed means you're moving at about twenty percent normal speed. I was there no doubt.

Kashi and I had been in New York City for about four months when I connected with a young lady I had been talking to very sparingly over the phone and online. Let's call her Ama (pronounced Ah Ma). Ama is a female deity in the Canaanite tradition that aligns with the planet Saturn. She governs death and the ultimate rebirth of life. Her favorite color is black and the emotion governing her power is depression.

I knew of Ama from my college days, but never talked to her at all. When we first reconnected we talked off and on for a while, a little chat here, a phone conversation there. We started making a solid connection with one another and it was good. Everything stayed pretty normal except for one conversation we had before I moved to NYC where I took her through a role-playing game to help her with her dating life. In this scenario, I met her in a lounge area and began to interact with her in such a way that she could feel her power and attractiveness as a woman. She had a powerful experience during that exercise, but so did I. Uh oh, I felt something shift in how I felt about her. Damn! I remember it like yesterday, I was on my way to see D-Train (see chapter *Best Pussy on the Planet* for D-Train's story) when we talked that night and the shift occurred. Did I seed her or me during the process? Maybe, I seeded the both of us. That's the thing about being a Tantra practitioner; you have to be strategic when seeding individuals so that you don't affect yourself in the process. The goal is to help them see themselves in a particular light, not so much yourself.

For those that don't know, that's what I do. I change women's entire vibration and consciousness so they can attract and keep a man for the long term if they so choose. As a matter of fact, there hasn't been a woman that I have dated (except for one) or taken through my set of processes who hasn't found her life partner. It's just what I do.

But following that process with her I realized I was affected. I can't explain exactly what shifted in me, but I felt it happen right there during that session. I felt more connected to her.

Fast forward to me living in NYC…

I received a call from Ama saying she would be in town taking care of some business and wanted to see if I had time for drinks. Of course I was down and not only was I down, but I was excited. So, that day arrived and I headed to the Delancey Street area to the hotel where she was staying and met her at the hotel bar.

- Soft, firm embrace that lasted about thirty seconds, but felt like a lifetime.
- Hair was soft, short, and well done.
- She was the perfect height and fit into me like saddle on a horse's back.
- Beautiful smile and face that snatched my heart right out of my chest before I could even speak to her.

I wasn't expecting that. For the hug to feel that familiar and good, that is. For her to embrace me like she was in love with me and I her. I didn't expect to fit together with her so well just like a hand and glove. Has that ever happened to you where you embrace someone and literally lose track of time and space? It was one of those hugs. I would experience this again with her before the night was through.

- Pomegranate martinis times número dos.

I'm not a big drinker, but I'm a drinker. What that means is I can drink because my liver works like it's on steroids, but I really haven't mastered the art of drinking. I can only name like ten mixed drinks so I usually order what everyone else is ordering. All that to say; I've got a very slight buzz happening after the second pomegranate martini.

- Pitch black lounge inside of this black colored hotel (interior and exterior) with black leather theme, couches, curtains, bar to match her black winter coat, black stockings, black leather boots, short black hair, perfectly painted black eye lashes and eye brows.

These are all what I call Ama significators because Ama's color is black, she's a she, and her environment and garb tends to be black as well. Under another circumstance the environment wouldn't have been so intoxicating, but this was just a cool vibe all the way around probably because of her. It was artistic and she seamlessly blended in to the surroundings. It's like she owned the hotel or at least designed the interior.

- Conversation is effortless.

Have you ever had the experience where conversation is easy and truthful, for the most part? You know, where minimal anesthesia – things we tell people so they feel okay and not hurt or emotional – is required when communicating with a person. Is that refreshing or what? To just be you. We're catching up on each other's past, but now it's like eleven at night and I'm ready to go. Hey, what'd you expect? I had no plans of having sex with this woman. First of all she had always come off very conservative, which is another Ama significator, and second of all I wasn't interested. I mean, this was my first time seeing her in like forever. Besides, I was looking forward to catching the subway trains before they slowed down going back to Harlem. I guess I was getting that New York state of mind, but needless to say, I stayed in the lobby with her and our conversation continued.

One Hour Later

I'm on the elevator with her heading up to her room and as soon as the elevator doors closed she rolled into my chest and buried her soft frame there with her head against my chest. It was that saddle horseback fit again. But she didn't bury her face in my chest she buried it in my heart. She penetrated my soul. I will never forget that. We didn't undress or have intercourse that night, but we did make love and shared our souls with one another. It was like we needed each other on a soul level. It was beyond physical. It was so strong that I professed my love for her that night. I must have left my nut sack in the lobby or something because I was very overwhelmed with feeling and emotion. I also felt as though I didn't need another woman in my life except for her. I was ready to cut everyone off the very next day. I HAD FALLEN IN LOVE WITH HER. It was the strongest feeling of love that I can remember. I was completely gone. Goodbye Kashi. Goodbye kids. That's what it felt like in that moment. I can still remember it specifically to this day.

As I mentioned, we didn't make love that night, at least not in the physical. We stayed fully clothed for the most part, but I make my connections energetically first and physically second if necessary. Once we got to her room we fell into each other on all levels. Her entire being surrounded me and I fell into her. We kissed so deeply it was like kissing her spirit. I could taste the lips of her inner goddesses.

By the morning time her and I were in the same space, but I was no longer a complete nutcase. I knew I wasn't going to leave my wife and kids, but everyone else was about to get cut and I mean before the day was out.

But this is not to celebrate a love story or even to talk about my experience with Ama. It's to synthesize this thing called LOVE and all its associated feelings and emotions. It's to understand what happens to the human mind when one "falls in love." Because I was there in that feeling place ready to cut people off and change my whole daily routine and I started the process of doing just that. I called Queen (see chapter "The Art of Subtle Touch" for my experience with Queen) and told her I didn't want to see her anymore. She was like, "*What the fuck are you talking about Rakhem?! Where's all this crazy talk coming from? This doesn't even sound like you.*" That break up actually wasn't successful, but it's the fact that I even made that call that showed me my state of mind after being with Ama.

Fall In Love

Is falling in love a good thing? I mean, is that a good place to be? It feels great half of the time and feels like getting the shit kicked out of you the other half. It's almost like getting the best head you can imagine three times a day for a week straight then having to roll around on broken glass three times a day for the next week. Being a metaphysician I understand the law of duality, which says for every high there must be an equal and opposite low and being in love seems to provide the highest highs and the lowest lows on the planet. Let's look at the phrase to see if there are any clues or warnings inherent there in.

FALL. Now when most people fall that shit is not pretty. It's funny to other people, but it's painful physically and mentally to the person experiencing it. I mean, who wants to fall? No one I know. I remember I was walking to an early morning class in college and seeing a guy trip and fall. His books were all over the place and no one slowed down to help him. But the thing was, he tried to maintain his balance and keep on his feet for like ten yards. You know when you trip and your falling forward so you try to run fast to get your legs under your now falling forward body, but that never works and you just look like a total clown who refuses to go down quietly and who would rather provide major entertainment for the surrounding spectators. Meanwhile as he's trying to avoid the inevitable fall he's kicking books and papers all over the sidewalk and what could have taken five seconds to happen has now taken twelve seconds. And instead of scraping a knee you've now incurred collateral damage like toe jams, busted lips, scraped knuckles, and a story in the school newspaper – "*Freshman busts his ass all the way up the north walkway on the way to class and brings laughter to students who would otherwise be stressed out about final exams.*" So the point is no one wants to fall, but also trying to avoid the fall just seems to make things worse.

IN. When we say 'IN' are we implying an enclosed space with certain definite boundaries? Like I walk IN the room. I rode IN the elevator. I got IN the car. The policeman put the criminal IN jail. She got IN trouble. I got all up IN that ass. The word IN is never used to describe freedom or expansion. It's used to describe some type of confinement.

Person A: "*Hello. I saw you sitting at the bar alone. Can I buy you a drink?*"

Person B: "*I'm sorry, I'm IN a relationship.*" – translation, "*I'm physically and mentally confined and unable to participate in certain activities regardless of whether I want to or not.*"

IN is confinement and OUT implies freedom. Like in Monopoly you select a "Get OUT of Jail FREE" card.

"*Where are the children?*"

"*They're OUT at the park.*" – unless the park has a fence then they are IN or at the playground.

So IN means confinement of at least your mind, but also could also include your body. Being IN a relationship is a mental confinement, but once the mind is trapped the body is sure to follow.

LOVE (noun). I'm tripping over this LOVE word as a noun, not a verb because loving someone is different than the state of being in love. We have to figure this out so let me just cut to the chase. LOVE is an emotional state that has the effect of INTENSELY pushing or pulling us toward a material object. That object could be money, a person, chocolate cake, I don't care what noun you stick in there, but it will be an object and the key is it's not a choice; it's an attraction or compulsion (a push or pull).

So back to our question – is falling in love a good thing? The answer is simple. Yes it's good if you want to grow past your involuntary attraction to material things. Yes it's good if you are in the driver's seat and allow yourself to fall in love and experience its wonder and magic. Yes it's good if you want to understand why you tend to fall in love with certain types of people versus the ones we know intellectually are better for you, but you have no attraction to. No, if you do it without awareness. No, if you desire to choose which direction you want to go in your life. I really do mean Yes and No here. The important thing is to properly acknowledge which answer best fits your situation. Good luck!

Getting the most from our sexuality involves an awareness of why our lover, wife, girlfriend, or friend with benefits is in our life and our true feelings towards them. We have to acknowledge that to ourselves and to them. That gives us the best chance to show up authentically as intimate and sexual beings and share and feel completely and in the moment. Not knowing this can leave us in the dark and feeling empty. If you're in love with your partner it will help you to understand what inside of you is drawn to them so that proper relationship expectations can be set. This is just some food for thought.

Oh, what of the depression you ask from the beginning of the story? Well, I had fallen in love with Ama; therefore, my world changed. What defines happiness, sadness, success, and failure had all been redefined for me. My physical and mental were in a sense now confined to a new world and set of rules. So that said, the very next day she said something to me that felt like it took the life out of me. If any other woman had said that including ones from past intense relationships I had been in, I wouldn't have given a crap about it. I maybe would have said to myself, "This *#%$ is crazy." But I didn't. I took in her words. I made them the gospel. I was wrong, bad, a villain, unworthy, a poor excuse, inconsiderate, and the list goes on. After she said it my body and brain basically shut down. I had to find a couch or a park bench and curl up for a few hours. I would be intensely depressed after that day for about four days, but lingering effects lasted for weeks. What did she say? It doesn't really matter, but it had something to do with not honoring the love I had professed to her. The point is what words out of someone's mouth should be able to make any-one feel like that? The point is that I had fallen into a emotional state and had no control or point of reference to the degree that one sentence out of her mouth could literally shut me down. But the opposite was true as well because she could also make me feel like ten billion dollars and did exactly that the night before. It's just the duality of it all.

It was definitely a growth experience for me and for that I am thankful for it.

CHAPTER 9

THE "GIRTHIEST"
(SIZE DOES MATTER)

A woman's expectation leading up to sex doesn't just affect the quality of her sexual experience, it determines it entirely. We create our lives.

How you present yourself in the mind of a woman is of grave importance in how you will connect with her and better yet, how she will receive you. If she thinks you are a stud then you'll be highly successful in that arena. If you come off as unsure, well the same applies. It's important to be that which you want and stay consistent in that behavior and in doing so you will win the minds of those you love and desire to bring pleasure.

♠

Is Brooklyn in the house? Yes indeed. The best thing about women is they will tell you all about yourself, both the good and the bad. Sometimes they are very direct and to the point and yet other times you need to read between the lines. But even when they make you read between the lines they are being pretty darn direct. Women are so sweet at that.

Man: "So baby, how was the sex?" *I know I put it down. She was loving that shit. I just want to hear her say it.*

Woman: *Hmm…how can I phrase this so he understands he's got some work to do without totally breaking his will to live?* "Yeah, well, only you can put it down like you be putting it down Big Daddy."

Man: *That was a bullshit response and she needs to come more direct than that, but let me play nice here and maybe get some more clarity.* "Ah, I see. So that's a good thing, right?"

Woman: *Ok, he didn't quite get everything I was saying, so let me ease in another subliminal indirect communication, but again with-*

out totally breaking him down. "You know no one is quite like you Big Daddy."

Man: *What the fuck is that supposed to mean? This is some bullshit.* "Ok, thanks."

Woman: *Ok, I think maybe he got it that time. Now let me figure out how to get out of here and call Jason so he can finish the job right. I'm still in need of some serious attention.*

That's actually how a lot of conversations go between people in relationships. There's what's said which represents a certain level of honesty and then there's what's not said, which represents the truth. Most couples can't really communicate and therefore problems persist and issues abound. That lack of communication also kills the sexual and intimate connection between them. But worse than that is the lack of authentic communication keeps things the same over time. Very little changes in a couple's intimate life. Part of the culprit is our expectations that the experience will be the same as it was last time even if we call ourselves hoping for the best.

I met the nicest young lady through a mutual friend. She was that really cool, street smart, quick on her feet, quick to tell you about yourself type who was really just a marshmallow on the inside. Just as sweet as she could be. Her and I had the chance to hang out a few times after we decided to barter each other's services. I provided her some tantric bodywork to help open her to feeling herself and achieving a deeper orgasm and she provided me with some massage and esthetics treatments. Very nice! The cool thing is after we would provide each other the service we would just hang out and talk, maybe listen to some music. I'm not sure about other men, but the livest feeling in the world is hanging with a beautiful woman whom you have no pressing interest in sexually. It just makes everything so easy and light. This was a situation where we were both cool with just being in each other's company. It's not that she wasn't attractive, because she was and she thought the same about me, but we were cool with just chilling.

All that said, we did eventually hook up a few months later and it was quite nice for both of us. But here's the thing, when I was standing there butt ass naked with my rock hard dick pointing at her she made a comment to effect of, "*Wow.*" She was basically saying I had a big penis, which is cool. I can accept that and appreciate her acknowledging such. Cock size never meant that much to me because I know that the size of the cock doesn't have anything to do with the quality of the sex. It does have a lot to do with how women are stimulated during sex, but a big cock is no better than a medium cock in reality. Not only that, but cock sizes adjust over time based on the size of the woman's pussy unless the man has some mental blocks, which many men do. I don't think there's any science behind that, but trust me it does. Especially, if you're having raw sex, meaning no condom so that the cock can actually feel the wet pussy walls.

I asked her what the "*Wow*" was for and she said, "*You're girthy.*" then proceeded to laugh to herself like you do when you luck up on a pleasant surprise. I said, "*Oh, yeah. I've heard that before. Is everything going to be cool?*" She said yes and nodded her head in agreement. In that very moment I knew she was going to have a good sexual experience with me that night. I could feel the tension in her body lighten up as some of the mystery of having sex with me for the first time disappeared.

We were both completely naked in a matter of seconds, but there was no rush to get into the bed. We both just moved with intent and with a steady pace. She pulled out a condom and handed it to me and watched me put it on as if to make sure it was put on correctly. We laid down in the bed together naked for the first time although it didn't feel like the first time with her. Maybe because of our Tantra session in her bed a few months earlier or maybe we were just two old souls reuniting for a time. She was so beautiful. Smooth skin all over her body with the prettiest lips in Brooklyn, guaranteed. They were rosy red with a thick pucker shape. They were the kind of lips that get drafted for lipstick or lip-gloss commercials. Her lips sat neatly under the cutest button nose and the keenest, roundest eyes I had seen in a while. Man, I really appreciate the beauty women possess. It's something to marvel at, but also something to whip the passion up within me. Her having distinct features seems to make my dick that much harder.

I softly touched her on the chest and glided my hand down her center to her navel, then to her side and up her side to her shoulder and breast. Her body was flawless and as such needed to be treated with care. It needed to be honored and touched appropriately. I leaned over to her and kissed her gently on her cheek, then even more gently on her lips and just held myself there until my lips melted into hers. I wanted to bond with her energy first. She had to feel both my intention and me that night. At this point my cock was so hard it was about to bust out of the condom and my own skin. It was like all the blood from my body was trying to fit in my dick.

After kissing and touching each other for a while I moved on top of her and in between her legs. Now, she was about 5'3" or so with a tiny, but very thick frame, but my penis was obviously much bigger than her vagina opening even though she was plenty moist. I leaned over her again and kissed her gently again so that she knew I was going to take my time and keep the same pace as our foreplay. I put the head of my penis at the opening of her vagina and pressed slightly so that she knew I was there and lined up to go inside of her. I pressed inside of her and then eased up to allow her to adjust to my size. I stirred a bit so that the motion never stopped, but made sure my entry was slow and steady. I pressed again and made more headway inside of her taking my time all the while. It took me about fifteen minutes to get my penis fully inside of her and once there I stayed still and continued to kiss her on her lips. I wanted to give her time again to adjust to me. Once she was comfortable I began to stir and grind slowly inside of her. There was no need to push in an out as she had a full stimulation from my penis being inside of her completely filling up her whole vagina. We made love steadily in that same way for the next hour and then stopped to hold each other. She told me, "*That's how it's supposed to be done.*" I was appreciative of her being open to me. It was a beautiful experience for both of us. Ten minutes later I was ready to make love to her again, but I remembered I wouldn't be able to stay hard the second time around with a condom on. I need to feel some wetness for sure after I've ejaculated once already.

About a week later when her and I were talking on the phone she told me she wished she didn't hold back on me. I guess I was confused by what she was talking about at first, but then assumed that she maybe wanted to give me head or something before we made love, but I really wasn't sure. It wasn't until about a year later that I fully understood what she had meant; I found out she was a Scorpio. I couldn't believe it. Although our sexual experience was beautiful the fact that she was a Scorpio and admitted to holding back told me things could have gone to a whole different level that night, but why didn't they? It didn't go to another level because her impression of me was of this nice guy. She didn't expect that I had a big dick, or that I could fuck, or that she would be into me afterwards and the reason was that I painted the nice guy picture in her mind.

What I realized is how a woman's expectations leading up to and during sex affect her actual experience. When a woman sees a big hard cock she has a tendency to assume it will be a fulfilling experience for her as opposed to seeing a real little penis the size of a roll of quarters. But when you talk with women who've been with a variety of partners they will tell you that men with smaller penises have provided some exceptionally orgasmic sex because their penis was able to hit extremely sensitive spots inside the vagina. The point here is that in reality although various size penises provide different feelings and sexual experiences in the end size doesn't matter as much as one would think. But impression and expectations in the minds of women do matter.

If a woman is open to you and believes you can put it down then she will more than likely have that experience. If she's not sure about it, then it probably won't be a great experience for her in the end. I think the same holds true for men, but to a lesser degree.

It's important for you to paint a picture for your woman before you engage her sexually and the sky is the limit for how you do this. It can be through the power of the word or by show and tell, but whatever you choose it needs to be sincere and convincing to be affective. If you don't paint a picture for her then she'll paint her own picture and there's no need to take that risk unless you have an idea of what she's thinking already. When Brooklyn saw my big hard cock it created a picture for her, an expectation. It sent her mind into a specific direction regarding how our sex was going to be and knowing is half the battle because the brain works hard to meet that expectation. When someone expects something of you they'll give you the benefit of the doubt until your consistent actions say otherwise. So in her mind is the nice, attentive, and gentle man with a big cock. The nice guy stuff ruled out any freaky sex, which is very normal and expected with Scorpios. Do you see how that played out for her?

I always tell my son to establish yourself as a straight "A" student in the minds of your teacher because they will give you the benefit of the doubt when it comes to giving you a final grade. They'll assume, for example, that if you weren't in school, it was for a legitimate reason as opposed to the "C" student who is assumed is being lazy or playing hooky.

And I'm not just saying this as a game to play with women because this is as serious as it gets and goes beyond sex. Based on the nature of the feminine, many women require a vision of the future and something to focus on. Like women say, "*I was looking forward to seeing you tonight.*" That means all during the day they held a vision in their mind of what the entire night was going to look and feel like once you got there. They've made love to you a thousand times already in their mind before you even get there. As a man engaging in a holistic sexual experience, you need to set these expectations and subsequently deliver on them. It's how you build trust in a relationship and help your woman have a fulfilling experience.

Parts is Parts

Being with a Scorpio woman means her ability to feel is limited and that's no exaggeration. She physically can't feel at the same level as say a Gemini can. This is my theory based on some astrological sciences I work with. What does that mean? It means that certain parts and activities are brought into play right off the bat: anus, hair pulls, neck grabber, hardcore breast massage with hard pulling of the nipples, pounding of the cock into the pussy, and spanking that ass like she stole your 401k savings. Don't look at me; that's just the law of being born in late fall. If you don't believe me just hit a dating site and request a Scorpio in your search criteria. When you get them in the sack watch how bored they are with the standard straight-up sex.

Scorpio Person: *"That was very nice, but next time can you grab my hair and spank me with that leather strap hanging on the wall. If I start bitching you can choke the shit out of me and shove your cock in my ass."*

I'm not saying that all Scorpios are like this or that other zodiac signs don't enjoy hardcore sex, but I have experienced this quite consistently with Scorpios. Either way, it does help to know the person you're with and what they desire sexually, which is why communication is key, especially, to get past the initial impressions and expectations we each may have.

THE "GIRTHIEST"

CHAPTER 10

TIME TO CUM

Even after I started educating myself about sex I still carried a belief that there was generally a period of time required to bring a woman to orgasm even if she was doing it on her own. I was wrong.

FOR ME THIS WAS a lesson about time. The chapters about phone sex and remote intimacy are more about space; the fact that physically being in the same space as your partner is not a requirement for deep connected intimacy and pleasure. Meaning, I can be half way around the world from my partner and still have a profound effect on her ability to feel pleasure and have an orgasmic experience even without contacting her through the phone. But the other aspect of the duality governing sexual interaction is the myth of time. How long does it take for you to experience deep connected pleasure when you are physically or energetically connected to someone? Or how about this, how long does it take for your woman to orgasm uncontrollably once your cock penetrates the vaginal cavity? Five-minutes? Fifteen? How about zero minutes?

♠

I hadn't seen Nita in almost two decades, but she was my first serious girlfriend ever and I was her first man, period. My time with her represented the first time in my life where I had sex every day. You know that saying cumming your brains out? Well, that's how it felt during a year when I was in a rigorous engineering curriculum and having fun in the sack. Consistent intercourse, consistent head, and loosing more semen than the law should allow. It was with Nita that I learned a lot about sex. I learned the difference between wearing a condom versus not wearing one. I learned and perfected how to pull out right before ejaculation. I learned about a woman's menstrual cycle and when and how it comes on and how it affects their moods first hand. I learned you can fuck on a woman's period and it makes not a damn bit of difference except one less usable towel for the bathroom. But the most important lesson I learned was that a woman's sex drive is truly insatiable. There's no end to that tunnel; to the madness and there's nothing you can do about it as a man. Fucking her harder, better, more frequently doesn't change a thing. You may buy yourself a day off here and there, but for the most part she'll keep on coming. I learned that women love sex even more than men and even more than cumming itself. I also learned that women do not sleep unless they are thoroughly sexed out. It's against their DNA structure or something. If they didn't just fuck hard and long then they can't sleep. If they are asleep and you walk in the room at three in the morning, they are not really asleep. They're waiting on you to fuck their brains out. I learned that women have to be put to sleep, especially if they have any kind of sexual energy running through their veins. It's just the way it is.

We were deeply connected starting from our late teenage years. As a matter of fact, I was sure her and I would be married some day, but I ended up going through a major depression after I graduated from school and broke off our relationship because of it. We lost touch for a while after I got married as I went deep into spiritual culture and kind of disappeared off the map from all my college and childhood friends for about ten years. All of my friends were wondering what had happened to me. They heard I changed my name to Raheem or something.

The Friend Peoples Conversation:

- *"What's his name now? Raheem or something, right? Is that Muslim?"*
- *"Isn't he a part of some religious cult? Man, he used to be so cool and then got sucked into some sort of religious extremism. Such a shame."*

- *"I heard he wears robes and shit and walks around chanting and burning incense. Is that true? I never would have thought he'd be a religious nut job when he graduated, but you never can tell nowadays. I know his mother must be devastated."*
- *"I heard they don't even celebrate Christmas. Can you imagine how tough that is on the children?"*
- *"Oh, here he comes. Just smile and act normal."*

The interesting thing was my young relationship with Nita showed me more about myself than I understood at that time. It was with her that my jealousy issues really came to the forefront. I started out being jealous of any man that she had dated before me. It caused me not to trust her and not to believe her. She would tell me something and I would second-guess it. I would go through this process where I would look into her eyes and try to get a feel for what the real truth was. It was sad. It was me. I was seeing insecurity and lack of self worth at a young age and not even recognizing it.

And that's the issue with these initial boyfriend girlfriend relationships taking place before marriage. All this stuff is happening due to our lack of development and lack of knowing who we are and we end up damaging others as a result. How did my lack of trust in her impact her future relationships? If the love of her life didn't trust her fully, who would?

When I connected with her on the phone for the first time in years I sensed those issues come up again. I had been open relating for a while and had the opportunity to deal with some of my jealousy issues so I was ready to work on them again here with her. And I was able to deal with most of them before we met again in person. We had the opportunity to catch up and talk about my life, wife, children, career, as well as her career and past relationships. It was during those conversations that I felt the jealousy come up and it was then I started working on myself. I mean, what is that, being jealous of an ex-boyfriend? That shit is nuts when you think about it.

Eventually, Nita and I did meet up again in person. One thing about her is she maintained her beauty. She has always had one of the coldest, smoothest bodies on the planet. It's one thing to be thick in all the right places, but another thing entirely to have an athletic disposition about it. Her legs, ass, feet, breasts, and natural hair were all on point. Plus, she maintained this feminine softness about her along with a beautiful smile and great personality. I can see why she was my first love.

The first time we saw each other again was me visiting her for the weekend and it was like no time had passed. The love we had once shared was there, intact, and unchanged. We talked like it was yesterday and touched like we were together. She was in love with me and I with her. It was nice to be back at that place with her again.

We went from the airport to the shower to the bed. It just flowed that way.

When I was in spiritual culture one of the head priests used to tell about going into a state of trance. He would say, once you've been in state of trance or deep meditative state, you can just go back there whenever you want to. You don't have to go through the formal breathing and posture techniques that you used when you were first attempting to go into trance. He said, "*Just go into trance.*" As he was telling me this I knew it was true and followed what he was saying, but implementing it was difficult at the time. The training we went through up to that point made the process of going into deep meditation so formal and technical. From the preparation before the meditation itself with diet, shower, oil, incense smells, colors of clothes, and the like. It was a whole process to make it happen. So to go from that formal technical process to now just going straight into trance at will was an adjustment. But doable, and I was able to do it.

So it begs the question, where is the source of the orgasm really? Is it in the size, shape, and movement of the cock? Is it in how open her mind is and how wet her pussy is at the time of intercourse? Maybe it's the words I say before we even get started. In my mind this is a chicken or the egg scenario. I always tell my clients that they own their orgasm. It's not subject to anything or anyone outside of them. I know that goes against conventional wisdom, but conventional wisdom isn't always wise. It's oftentimes just traditional belief, and seeing as there are no absolute truths, what was a truth yesterday can become a fallacy today.

When Nita and I had sex the first time that night it was unlike anything I had experienced before which was surprising because we had been together so many times before. I took my shower when we got to her house and found her on the bed with her beautiful body calling me to her. I climbed on her bed then climbed on top of her. She opened her legs to allow me into her. I looked her straight into her eyes the entire time as I guided my penis to the entrance of her vagina. As soon as I pushed inside of her she started to orgasm uncontrollably. Her body shook like she was having a seizure of some sort. It seemed to move in an "S" shape back for a long time. I could look into her face and tell that it was just a bit of surprise to her and that there was some discomfort with her being that vulnerable in front of me. But there was nothing she could do about it or wanted to do about it. I continued to push inside of her until my cock was all the way inside of her, and just slow grinded inside of her, but with very little movement because obviously it wasn't required.

I had been with a number of women where my movement

inside of them wasn't necessary to bring them pleasure during sex and eventually orgasm. And as a rule, I began to learn the less movement the better when it comes to a woman's deep pleasure during sex.

For me it was like an out of body experience with Nita. I felt that a part of me was just watching her and in the meantime I couldn't feel my body at all. It was like I wasn't really present in the experience, but just the observer. I've noticed that happens to me when I experience something surprising and unexpected. The same thing happened to me when I was rear-ended while sitting in my car at an intersection. As soon as I got hit time seemed to slow down for a while and I just observed myself for a moment before waking up pinned against the steering wheel. And the interesting thing about it is I've had the experience of initiating a woman's orgasm by just touching her and other times by barely touching her, but it was a surprise either way. The other thing was I've seen women orgasm like that during sex with me, but it was after some time had passed.

How long does it take to bring a woman to orgasm, or from her perspective, how long does it take to have one? My Tantra teacher said a woman could have an orgasm every one-eighth of a second for hours, but I never heard him say how long it took to bring a woman to one. I'll let him know to upgrade his statement and say that a woman can have an orgasm every one-eighth of a second from the time you engage her until the end of all eternity.

TIME TO CUM

CHAPTER 11

SOUTHERN BELLA

Sometimes blessings are too good to be true.

At some point in your life you have to let it all go. *Give it 2 The Sky* as Robin Thicke would say. Go all in. For me, giving it to the sky and letting it all go, meant reaching my utmost ability to feel whether it be pleasure, pain, or whatever came my way. The maximum openness and vulnerability I have felt to date was with my Bella. What it represents for me was a total release and acknowledgement of all that is good and great about the pussy. All that is great about the energy of a woman and how it can take everything that is wound up in a man and turn it into a garden of fruitfulness. Ashe!

What I've found is in order for me to do my work as an Integrated Intimacy and Tantric practitioner I have to go all in with women. You have to feel how they feel and experience the depths of their love to know their potential. It's the only way. The only problem is you have to maintain your consciousness and awareness so that you can pull yourself out; otherwise, you could get lost. My spiritual teacher used to say you must exit your meditation fully and in the right way or you don't become fully awake. A part of you stays in perpetual meditation and you don't even know it.

My relationship with Bella was just that. It was an all-in, all-or-nothing type of love affair. It was where I learned it was okay to lose myself in love and that in the end things would be alright. It's where I learned to honor my partner and feel her pain. It's where I experienced what "blow your mind" sex felt like, not because the moves or positions were dope, but because I was all-in. We fucked with our hearts, minds, and spirits and nothing on earth really mattered in those moments. It's where I developed my skin-is-in and pulling-out-is-for-punks ruleset.

Shoes off Upon Entry

Let me say that when Bella and I came together to make love there was no foreplay. The only foreplay we did was the five seconds of feeling one another's body skin before my cock hit the entrance of some of the tightest, wettest pussy the world has ever seen. I bear witness. May I have a witness, because I've never witnessed anything quite like this, and I've witnessed a lot, my friend?

But here's the thing. Our cock to pussy ratio was off. As was stated earlier, I bring mad girth to the table when it comes to the bang-bang-get-down and Bella had the fattest pussy you ever could see, but she was still five feet two inches tall whereas I'm six feet three inches. So needless to say there was going to be some work involved to get my cock inside of her. Now let me stop here for a second and state the obvious question. Why not just use lubrication? Well, there was no need for lubrication. Over the years I had developed a technique that allows me to insert my cock into the tightest of pussies. I've never been able to not get into a pussy. Never. The technique involves me using the woman's wetness and involves a series of baby in-and-out and up-and-down strokes that thoroughly wet her pussy all the way around both inside and out while at the same time thoroughly lubricating my cock. Literally, within no time I'm all the way in there. It's a technique that I intuited back in college and a thing of beauty to behold.

So what was the problem here? The problem, or in this case the blessing, was that as soon as my cock hit the entrance of Bella's pussy I was instantly paralyzed for lack of a better word to describe it. I no longer had conscious control over my body in the same way. I was being driven by spirit and energy as opposed to my conscious thinking desires. This feeling was the experience of going straight into a full-body orgasm (not ejaculation) and this orgasm lasted for the entire fifteen minutes or so it took me to get all the way inside of her. Now, I know a lot of men have not experienced an orgasm before, but only ejaculation, and for those individuals let me help you understand this feeling.

First of all, have you seen a women have a vaginal or full-body orgasm? This is not clitoral; meaning localized to the clitoris, but full-body in nature. You can tell because their whole body goes into convulsions that looks similar to an epileptic seizure. Not only that, but they don't have a sense of where the orgasm is coming from. They're looking around in a state of confusion while trying to grasp anything sturdy enough to hold their weight. It's like an invisible octopus is tickling eight parts of your body at one time with varying degrees of intensity and you can't focus on any of them and all of them at the same time. There is no conscious control, but rather raw energy moving wherever it can, which if you're healthy, is throughout the entire body. Imagine feeling an intense rush up your spine, neck, base of your brain, then shooting through your ass crack into your thighs then back into your shoulder blades, back down your spine into your nut sack. Imagine trying to speak, but instead you just slobber uncontrollably like a stroke victim into the pillow. Look here, I know a number of people spend a lot of time trying to cum, but when you are having a full-body orgasm your mind is focused on stopping cumming. Like when is this lightning going to stop going from the crack of my ass, up my spine to the base of my brain and back down into my nut sack? Never? Ok, cool. I'll just keep drooling into the mattress and hope my girl is not planning an exit strategy to get this nutjob off of her.

Me (after our sex is done): "*Yeah baby, I think I was having an orgasm when I was going crazy there.*"

Bella: "*Oh, okay. Wow, that's great. Well, I guess you better go now because I have to ah…ah…feed the dog. Yeah, and he likes to eat in private or else he gets real cranky and stuff. But I had a great time and I'm looking forward to seeing you again in another lifetime, I mean, real soon.*"

Me: "*I see. I guess that freaked you out a bit.*"

Bella: "*What? No. It was great. Well, let me get these Kibbles and Bits.*"

I can see how that conversation would go with her girlfriends.

Bella: "*Yeah girl. He was like shaking and shit and wasn't even inside of me yet. I was like I know this brother ain't cumming already. Damn!*"

Girlfriend: "*Wow. Did he cum like that?*"

Bella: "*No. It's like the cum was trapped in his nut sack or something. I mean he was trying to get it out and shaking and moaning. His eyes rolled up into his head like he caught the Holy Ghost or something. But the nut was stuck so he just kept on shaking and carrying on. I was like, 'Hello, hello, don't forget about me down here under your crazy shaking ass.' I was like what the fuck?*"

Girlfriend: "*I know that's right girl. Get that freakshow up off you and call Dwayne. I told you to stick with those brothas who be laying it down right.*"

Bella: "*Exactly! Then when the nut never came out he wanted to keep fucking me. I was like and go through another epileptic seizure in about five minutes? No thanks. 'Um, I gotta feed the dog.' I had to shake my self a few times so he thought I came and slide from under*" *that negro. Ewww, yuck. I should post some shit on Facebook about this shit. Wasted a good Friday night messing around with a man trying to catch the Holy Spirit on top of me.”*

Girlfriend: *“Yeah girl. Post that shit.”*

Bella: *“It was like a horror movie or something. Did you see that movie* Alien *when that creature bust up out the man's chest and squirmed across the dinner table? That's all I could think of in the moment when he was convulsing on me. I was like is an alien about to bust out of his chest and eat me alive in my own bedroom. What did I do to deserve this shit? Girl as soon as he left I locked the whole house down, deadbolted the door and drank like three glasses of wine and got my vibrator and got a real piece and went to sleep.”*

Say what? I can't go out like that. But those are the kinds of thoughts you have when you're a man having an orgasm that looks like a woman's orgasm. But that's my point; the full body male orgasm is a perpetual state of vulnerability for a man. It allows him to empty and express the heart and soul of who he is. Plus, it feels really good and lasts a long time. It can wear you out if your not careful.

So when I hit the entrance of Bella's pussy I was unable to use the technique because I was unable to think. Instead my instinct was to just push forward into the pussy which believe it or not was not the most efficient way to get in there. My cock entered her slowly and each push felt like an orgasm all in its own. Half way through this process I had to bury my head in the pillow and tell myself everything was going to be okay. As a matter of fact, that's what I said over and over.

“Okay. Okay. Okay. Okay. Okay.”

I literally couldn't say anything else. Actually, I think I said "*God,*" a few times and "*Jesus*" a few times too. But you get the picture.

Something else needs to be said because this is a concern I had during the orgasms with Bella. These orgasms were so intense that I thought I may ejaculate, but I never did. It's not that I had the feeling of wanting to ejaculate, but rather, thinking my brain or nut sack or whatever would automatically associate this intense pleasure with ejaculation and make it happen through association or something. But as I said, it never happened. This was true across the board even with women other than Bella. I would have similar orgasmic experiences, although not as intense, but they never lead to ejaculation. So that proved to me that these experiences were not related other than they are both energy-based and felt great. An ejaculation is the movement of energy out of the body while the orgasm is the movement of energy inside of the body. Ejaculation is a masculine expression of pleasure while orgasm is feminine one. Orgasm brought out emotions in me that I would usually witness with the women I would be with like crying. It was during my orgasmic experiences that I first cried during sex.

Once I got all the way inside of her the intense orgasms stopped or at least lessened in intensity. At that point what we had more so resembled standard fucking even though it was still very different. It was mostly grinding with slight movements or it was me being still while she rode me from the bottom. I called it "bottom riders" because I would just be still while she moved her body around until she came to orgasm. I had actually gotten that from a few women who said I didn't have to move at all for them to have intense pleasure with me during sex. It's not as easy as it seems though. It's tough for a man to be still during sex even when he's on the bottom.

Audio & Video Sex

For the first time in my life I've been satisfied with phone sex to the point where I didn't want physical sex. As in I'm good. Like really. And the thing is, it's not based on the fact I ejaculated and now I'm chilled out. It based on the fact that the experience was so intense and the orgasm (not ejaculation) was so intense that I needed to go to sleep afterwards. That's the thing about being energetically open; it can be extremely intense.

I was never really into masturbation growing up. For one, my friends really looked down on masturbation. A few boys I knew growing up got caught masturbating in their homes and got teased relentlessly in school. Not only were they teased, but also that canceled them out from getting anywhere close to some pussy. I mean, no friends, nothing. People wouldn't even shake hands with these dudes. I bought into that mindset, but I still snuck and masturbated a few times in my room. I was too horny not to and wasn't getting any pussy whatsoever. None! I do remember ejaculating felt good, but at the same time, I felt guilty afterwards.

When I started dating Bella we were able to satisfy most of our intimacy needs just through talking on the phone, but that didn't last long. Eventually, we both needed more, but in the meantime it was a totally fulfilling experience to have energetic sex with her over the phone. It started with her, and I would lead her through a phone intimacy session so she could feel more connected to me. It went something like this.

Me: Where are you at right now?

Bella: I'm in my room, laying on the bed.

Me: Nice. I like that. What are you wearing?

Bella: T-shirt and panties.

Me: Ouch, that hurts. It's sounds like you're way over dressed. (Sigh) I'm really sad about that.

Bella: LOL. Is it really that bad, baby? I can take off the t-shirt. (Takes off t-shirt)

Me: That's a good start. (Sigh)

Bella: Okay, I'll take my panties off too. (Takes off panties)

Me: That feels so much better. How do you feel now?

Bella: I feel good.

Me: I've been thinking about your body all day today. I like how smooth your skin feels, especially, your legs, stomach, and breasts. I want you to take a deep breath in when I count from three to one. When I say breathe in, I want you to breathe in through your nose and breathe out through you mouth and when you breathe in I want you to push your stomach out and when you breathe out bring your stomach in. Okay?

Bella: Okay.

Me: 3-2-1. Breathe in. Hold. Breathe out. Ready? Again, breathe in, hold, and breathe out. One more time, breathe in, hold, and breathe out. Good. Now just relax and breathe normally. What I'm going to do next is project myself into your room. I need a part of me to be there with you. I want to feel your energy and body as best I can. Is it okay if I do that?

Bella: Yes.

Me: (Waits thirty seconds so that I can project my energy into her room). I want you to feel me sitting on the edge of your bed. I'm on your right side. I'm looking into your pretty face and holding my hand about six inches above your clitoris. I'm just taking a minute to connect with your energy. Can you feel me in the room with you?

Bella: Yes.

Me: I can feel the energy rising from your pussy. Open your legs slightly for me.

(5 seconds pass). Is it ok if I lay next to you?

Bella: Yes. (I can feel her start rubbing her clitoris, breasts, and vaginal lips)

Me: I don't have any clothes on. I want to feel your body against mine. I'm going to put my leg over top of yours and place my hand on your stomach. While I'm doing that I'm kissing you very gently on your ear… and your cheek … and your neck… and now I'm taking my hand and moving your face towards me so I can kiss you very gently on your soft lips. I love how your lips taste. Keep your mouth closed while I lick you gently between your lips. Your lips taste like strawberry-flavored honey. Ok, now you can open your mouth and connect your tongue to mine, but I only want you to touch my tongue. Just make it available to me; I'll do all the work. While I'm kissing you gently, I'm caressing your face with my hand… and moving it down to your neck… then down to your breasts.

I'm squeezing your left breast. Your left nipple is in the center of the palm of my hand and I'm squeezing your breast, but don't stop kissing me. Focus on me. Look at me in my eyes while I look into yours. Feel the love I have for you. Feel the passion I have for you. Can you feel me?

Bella: Yes.

Me: Do you love me?

Bella: Yes.

Me: Can you feel my hard cock against the side of your right leg?

Bella: Yes.

Me: Grab my cock with your right hand. Hold it in your hand. Feel how hard it is, how smooth it is. I want my cock inside of you. But, I have to know you want me inside of you. I have to feel the passion you have for me.

Bella: Baby, I want you inside of me. Please.

Me: Open you legs wider for me. I'm going to move between your legs, but I want to taste you first. I'm kissing you on your stomach, playing with your navel and working my way down to your clit. I'm licking around your clit, but I'm not touching it. Now I'm licking and kissing all around your vagina… the inside of your right leg… your right ass cheek… across the crack of your ass… your left ass check… and the inside of your left leg.

I can feel the wetness of your pussy. It's like a vacuum pulling my tongue towards it. I'll start at the bottom of the opening of your pussy and lick up and inside of you… and I do it again going even deeper with my tongue. I grab both of your ass cheeks and pull your pussy into my face so that my tongue can be even deeper inside of you.

The tips of my fingers are tickling your anus. I'm licking each of your pussy lips and now I'm gently kissing and sucking your clit. My mouth is slightly open and I'm making love to your clit so gently. I'm surrounding your clit with my mouth and swallowing your essence into my mouth.

I love drinking you. I love loving you. I'm in love with you. You are the love of my life and my girl, my goddess. I'm still tickling your anus with the tips of my fingers… still squeezing your ass and still pulling you to me. Can you feel me?

Bella: YES!

Me: I want my penis inside of you. Do you want me inside of you?

Bella: YES!

Me: I'm giving you one last kiss on the clit and moving up the center of your body until my face is even with yours. Reach down and grab my cock. Guide it to the dead center of your pussy. Keep me right there at the entrance of you. Can you feel the head of my penis throbbing and ready to push inside of you?

Bella: YES!

Me: I'm pushing inside of you right now. Damn, your pussy is wet. It feels like liquid silk. The head of my penis is inside of you. I want you to feel the pressure of it filling up the entire entrance of your pussy. I'm kissing you on the lips and looking you in your eyes. I'm in love with you. You can see how much I want you when you look into my eyes. You can see how good you feel by looking into my face.

I'm pushing inside of you and now I'm halfway inside of you. My penis is filling up your entire vagina. There is no part of you that can't feel me inside of you. I'm kissing you on the lips and now I'm laying on top of your body. Feel my weight on top of you as I reach down to grab your ass with both of my hands. I'm pulling your ass apart to open you up even wider for me. I'm pushing all the way inside of you now.

I am completely in you. You can feel my dick expanding inside of you, growing, and widening and pressing against your walls. Can you feel me totally inside of you?

Bella: YES! (still massaging her clit and breasts, about to hit orgasm)

Me: I'm beginning to grind slowing inside of you and I want you to move with me. I want you to grind with me. Kiss me baby and look me in my eyes. Feel my weight pressing into you and against you as I'm still squeezing your ass and fingering you in and around your anus.

Bella: Oh, Rakhem, Rakhem, Rakhem… I'm cumming, I'm cumming…(deep moans of passion).

Me: I love you so much. You sound so beautiful to me. You are everything to me.

Bella: Shit! (Out of breath, laying back)

She would always feel me so strongly and have stronger and stronger orgasms the more we had phone intimacy even getting to the point where she would have multiple orgasms. In the beginning, these sessions were mostly for her. She would have the orgasm and I would hold her (virtually, of course) and be there for her. Her orgasms were so beautiful; just the sounds of her voice were reward enough for me.

After a number of months things started to change. She would hold me with her energy and bring me to orgasm and then to ejaculation. I couldn't believe it the first few times this happened. She would use her seductive voice to penetrate my soul and guide me to a state of ecstasy. This was possible for a few reasons: (1) she had this confidence in herself and her abilities to affect me energetically and (2) she knew she could have an orgasm whenever she wanted. It was no longer this elusive reality, but something totally under her control. Something she could play with. Tell me, how does sex change for a women when their orgasm is effortless and guaranteed whether it's phone sex or physical intercourse? Her whole attitude changes, that's how. She becomes a confident sex goddess and begins to wield her power during sex. She begins to focus on me, healing and strengthening me. At first it was scary because I realized that she was in control. She had me and I loved it. I surrendered to her power. I trusted her in everything I did.

As she told me, "*I got you, baby.*" I remember thinking to myself, "*Shit! What the fuck is happening?*" I found the perfect way to touch myself and how to grip my penis. There was no jerking and intense rubbing required. All I had to do was hold myself in a certain way and fall into her words and the sound of her voice. It wasn't long before I started going into orgasm. My body started convulsing. The environment around me changed. The light through the window looked different. The things I could hear in the background suddenly faded out. The world around me began to shrink and the room and bed became my entire universe. I was moaning and moving involuntarily, feeling like a puppet in a play and loving every second of it. Not knowing how long I would be in this state. My conditioned self wanted to be back in control, but at the same time I didn't want to assume control. The sensation was intense everywhere; my penis, legs, back, chest, you name it. Moving my legs didn't help change the feeling, but they continued to move uncontrollably as if they were trying to swim to shore.

I would eventually get to a point where I would ejaculate, but only because she wanted me to go there. She could feel my progress towards ejaculation and knew what to say to bring me closer and closer. I knew there was no escaping it. I was surrendered to her and trusted in her goddess power.

There were many times when we entered an orgasmic state together and would both be convulsing uncontrollably. We would be suspended in each other's energy, love, and presence.

These experiences were so intense that I didn't want to have physical intercourse. I was so incredibly satiated and satisfied it kind of scared me. I began to question the purpose of physical sex besides procreation. What's the point when you can feel this good without even touching one another. In other words, when the energetic connection between two people is this powerful why even resort to the physical connection?

These vulnerable experiences are a requirement for men. We need a time to release and let go without being in control of the situation. We need to know that our lovers have got us and will care for and heal us as men. Yes, most of the time we need to be in control and present as men, but there has to be a part of the day where we can relinquish control. It helps us appreciate what control and presence is and how our partners feel when we are in a controlling position. It's in those moments where we understand the "vulnerability" of surrender and will wield our power in a responsible manner. In the corporate world they say a good leader was first a good follower. Why? Because a leader understands the view and plight of the follower and will therefore lead accordingly.

It also provides us with the ability to purge anything that we held onto throughout the day or week. Yes, most times men don't internalize what we see and hear. We let it go right away; thus, the reputation for being cold and heartless creatures. But the reality is we hold on to a lot more than we would care to acknowledge and through this release and surrender we are able to purge those things from our minds and body. It's mandatory.

The Immaculate Nani

My initial story for Bella talked about the immense orgasmic pleasure I received during entry into her pussy. But that story didn't talk much about the pussy itself and how good it is once inside. The bottom line is it was good all the way around. Just wet, tight, nice. No matter which way you slice it or which position your in, it's the bomb and for me that's special because I've never really looked at a woman's pussy being good in and of itself because I've always looked at the complete experience with a woman. But this pussy was good.

But here's the thing. I was again able to achieve intense orgasm when Bella would ride on top of me or when I was making love to her from the back. This time it wasn't the entry inside of her that provided the orgasms, but the actual feeling of being completely inside of her as well. I once told her that her pussy felt better than head. Now that's a serious compliment because head is like a million dollars for a man – something tight and wet with zero work on our part. Just sit back and get you dick sucked until you cum in the girl's mouth then take a nap. It's just the ultimate form of worship and honoring of a man because you're communicating so much to him in this act, especially when it's done with care and attentiveness. It's like saying, this one's for you. Or I love you so much and I'm going to show you just how much. Head is for champions. But baby, instead of head you can just ride my joint. Nice!

When Bella rides me I immediately go into orgasm. However, I am a bit more in control during this orgasm. I have to be so that I don't toss her off of me and out the fucking window. I need to be mindful because she is so fragile on top of me and I need to allow her to maintain control because during this orgasmic state I can easily usurp control of our session, but I don't want to do that. Actually, it would be more beneficial if I was chained to the bed when she road me. She would have to chain my wrists, ankles, chest, waist, head, neck, toes, feet, and thighs to the bed. Yes, all of that to prevent me from rising up out that motherfucker. Because the point there would be to totally let go and just allow the orgasm to take over my whole body.

Here's the thing that should be noticed though. When she is riding me I still employ a level of control and awareness during my orgasms and as a result they are not as intense. In addition, the orgasms in this position do lead to ejaculations whereas the missionary positions don't. The point is that orgasm is a letting go process. When I coach women I emphasize this point. If you want to reach your highest orgasmic potential then you must let go. Stop thinking. Stop controlling and allow. Just allow. I will work to get to that point with Bella. I will have to quell my concerns that I may be too out of control or too rough for her small frame during my orgasmic experience with her on top of me.

Learning to Express – Male Vulnerability

Bella had taught me to be vulnerable. This was one of the most powerful loves I had known to date since being open and part of my growth was learning to express myself fully and publically in the moment. To do this meant I had to be in touch with my feelings and accept them as the truth of who I am. I wrote an essay to my love that went like this…

This is an acknowledgment of love. An opening of my heart and an escape from the self built barriers that hold me captive to my own feelings, desires, and self. This is about the love I have found with Bella.

I've never written about love in the present. Conversely, it's always been about the pain of the past or looking to a better future. As if somehow I've been hypnotized into believing that the present happiness isn't worthy of sharing. Or to share something great will ultimately lead to its demise in the future.

This year I met one of the all time great loves of my lifetime. I can honestly say that even in this youthful stage of my life. A love so beautiful and sublime that although I recognized it, I could have never hoped to fully appreciate it because it's ultimate purpose was to help me see my own specialness. A specialness within that I hadn't acknowledged or accepted. A love so easy that my disbelief in the effort-

lessness of life tried to push it away. Could it really be this easy and effortless and feel this good? It was hard to fathom.

How It Feels

When I'm with Bella, whether talking on the phone or in her presence, all other realities melt away for me. I find myself in a place without time or space. Although the immediate surroundings may have noticeable qualities to them, like a king size bed with golden colored linen sheets and a red throw comforter, faintly open blinds allowing the minimal light to stream through, a white dresser with a mirror that has so often held the reflection of my love's beautiful face and smile, the sounds of the TV off in the distance; everything outside those walls are nonexistent and immaterial. Is it possible to find a whole Universe in one person? How about heaven? To get lost in the infinite? I would say yes because I am experiencing that with her everyday.

No Words

Sometimes it's the poetry and sweet words that are said to us that make us feel good. Sometimes it's even just the sound of someone's voice that can take you there, but in this case it's her energetic presence that brings me peace, calm, and happiness. Just the knowledge that she is there has a profound effect on my psyche, my soul. I can feel her from one thousand miles away. When we are on the phone no words are necessary. I love that. The silence is not only comfortable, but reassuring and often times preferred. "Can I just sit on the phone with you?" I would like your strong stillness that feels so much like love to take me to sleep. To initiate the lucid dreams of us holding hands in a field of yellow flowers under a blue sky.

Being in Bella's presence for me is like being surrounded with a light that glows softly. It's cool and serene. It feels like the essence of love. Love without movement or sound. Just love. It makes our eight-hour conversations feel like eight minutes and eight lifetimes at the same time. It makes the last time we were together seem like an eternity. It makes me long for her. Search for her in the cosmos of my mind. To what do I owe the pleasure and to whom do I thank? Why have I attracted this blessing into my life? Who do I thank? She is to me like water is to the ocean. She surrounds me, consumes my being and for that I am grateful and thankful. She is me. She reflects everything that is special about myself and for that gift from the universe I am thankful.

In my life I have been who I've been. Both a jack and master of many trades. A believer in many things including the ultimate divine that precedes the Alpha and supersedes the Omega. But my relationship with Bella has allowed me to know myself more so than all of my experiences. The clarity is unmatched. The feeling is pure. Have you ever asked how? Why? You've attracted the blessings you have. Why did this flower appear in my yard? Why the check in the mailbox? It's because you are deserving of such. It's because it is you. It's okay to see the beauty in yourself reflected by someone else. I have seen that in Bella and am ever grateful and thankful.

This is why I love her.

Transcendental Love Making

Have you ever made love from across the room? How about from across the country? Sometimes circumstance, like a long distance relationship, can breed specialness beyond measure. Have you ever felt someone so deeply that it changed your consciousness, your very way of thinking, feeling, and seeing in that very moment? Have you ever orgasmed uncontrollably while in the rapture of the essence of another even when they weren't physically there with you? I have. I have felt the intense pleasure of her love moving through every cell in my body until my thinking mind releases control of all that it has known and protected. This is how it feels when we make love on the phone. An experience so intense it questions the need for a physical experience. Really. I literally don't want the physical experience afterward. From one perspective it almost feels shallow after transcendental lovemaking. It's so satisfying that I want to bask in its afterglow and not let go.

When we make love from a distance it allows me to release the tears and emotions that well up in men. Those emotions that have nowhere to go. No route for escape. Trapped in our beliefs about manhood and masculinity, but so desperately wanting to be released. For my love making with Bella whether transcendental or physical crying has become a common expression for me. Not always the tears, but the expression and release. The emotion of sadness and joy intertwined and with it the orgasmic pleasure that lasts throughout and after.

We are complete...

Having a Voice

What I learned to be of utmost importance is having a voice during sex and intimacy. Often times early in my sexual history I would be silent and hold in any expression of pleasure even during ejaculation. What I realized later on is that me holding in my natural expression during sex was mostly a result of a feeling of shame I felt around sex itself. I think a lot of people are in that same predicament where at least on a subconscious level they view sex as a shameful act and should therefore at the very least hold in their voice during the act. You know, do it in a quiet, dark place late at night when everyone else is asleep. Pretty much the same way we treated masturbation when we first explored our own sexuality, on the downlow.

It's interesting because all of my young sexual life I never knew I was suppressing how I really felt during sex. Part of it was a macho thing and how I thought a man was supposed to be in bed. Being strong, powerful and unfeeling. Meanwhile it's the woman who is supposed to make all the noise as a result of my strong and powerful love making abilities. There were also the times when I held in my sounds of pleasure because I didn't want the woman I was with to know I ejaculated. It's something about when a woman knows you've ejaculated that changes the whole experience from that point forward. I would experiment with it every once in a while to see if it really was a change in me phys- ically sixty-seconds after a nut or if it was her expectation based on my ejaculating. I did this with women who would normally just stop after I ejaculated and found that the silence does help. Some women, who insisted the sex changed immediately after I ejaculated, wouldn't notice a difference at all as long as I didn't say anything. They would even say how strong I was after I had already ejaculated. I would be laughing to myself whenever that happened because it just proved my point that expectation plays a huge role in sex and how much our mentality and expectation influences our sexual experiences. See the chapter, *The Girthiest*.

When I was with Bella I felt free for the first time in my life to completely express how I felt in the moment regardless of what else was happening. My "freedom" of expression was linked to my level of growth and confidence with my own sexual nature as well as being accepting of who I am and how I express myself. For example, there were times I wouldn't express my pleasure during ejaculation if it happened before my partner had an orgasm. Or other times when I wouldn't express my pleasure during orgasm (not ejaculation) because of how I thought it would be interpreted. The bottom line is it was easy for me to get caught up in my head. My relationship with Bella had exercised all of those suppressive thoughts and feelings. From one standpoint I felt as if I was having sex for the first time in my life. It was a totally freeing experience and it facilitated me having very long and intense orgasms, sometimes lasting for twenty to thirty minutes at a time. That was the last piece for me, which allowed me to truly master my orgasm; it was the expression along with the letting go. Is this the highest level for me to go? No, it's not, but it does represent a significant step in my development.

And She Sings

One thing I learned about is the importance of the sounds of our voice in making love. Expression of how you feel in the moment is the key to experiencing sex fully. Bella's voice was just about enough to send me into an orgasmic state by itself. Earlier I discussed being able to express oneself in sound and action, but equally important is the specific sound itself. Tone, pitch and whatever other musical terms apply to defining what one's voice actually sounds like is key.

What I eventually began to realize was that Bella would take care in how she addressed me; not only what she said, but also the tone and pitch of her voice. I used to think she did it naturally and to a degree she does, but she was also intentional with it. For me it was important because it relaxed me and put my entire body at ease. Once that took place I would oftentimes find myself aroused and wanting to be with her physically or energetically if we weren't with each other because of our distance. It was like Bella was singing to me in a beautiful melody that soothed my soul. It became a necessity in my life. The same applied during out lovemaking. It was the sound of her voice that cracked my outer shell and allowed me to be fully open and in the moment with her.

Truth versus Honesty

If I were to be honest I would say I had one of the deepest loves I've ever known with Bella. That she was critical to my life on so many levels it's even hard to quantify. In all honesty, I was deeply in love with her. No ifs, ands, or buts about it. But what is honesty? Honesty is the very real assessment of the feelings and emotions running through your very being at a particular time. It's how you honestly feel. What you honestly see with complete and total presence, leaving nothing out. That's honest, right? But, what I see and how I interpret it is influenced by my perspective, by my ego and we know our perspective and ego change over time based on our cumulative experiences. So again, we are defining honesty based on how we see things based on our perspective at a particular time. This is far from what I would call truth or an absolute truth.

So then what is truth? Well, to understand truth we need to understand the duality of our beings. We need to understand that there is our ego and our self where the self is a constant indifferent part of our being that has the potential to know and experience all things without being attached to any of it. I know that sounds super metaphysical, but that's the best way to describe it. There's your personality or ego and your independent observer and both have an influence in your life, but interpret it completely differently.

The diagram below attempts to depict the ego and the self, including their actual relevance in our life as indicated by the size of each circle.

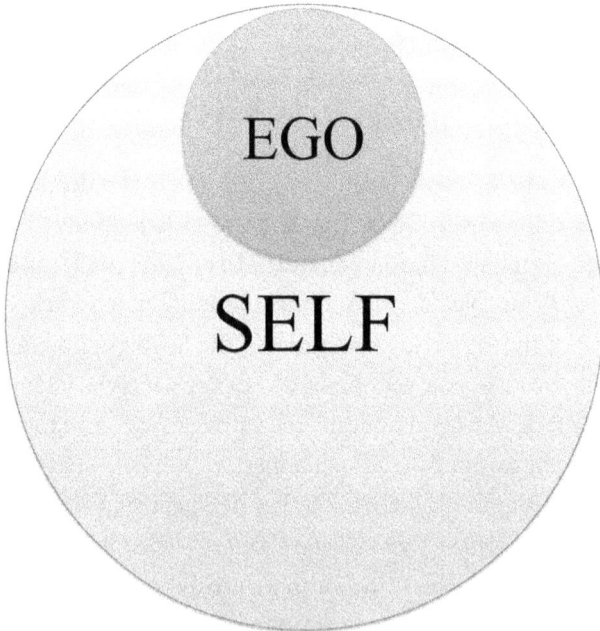

EGO

SELF

So, back to this elusive truth. If I honestly felt one of the deepest loves I've ever known then what is the truth of the situation? The truth is that Bella reflected in me a number of things that were required for me to advance in my growth. First, she reflected in me the need to step into my highest level of personal expression. Bella was closed in many ways. She refused to step outside of her comfort zone and express her unique talents in the world. She was caught up in blaming others and I was in the same predicament. I deeply desired to move into my highest expression, but had thoughts and beliefs that held me back. I had to get out of my shell, but I actually loved that about her and myself. That quietness backed up with the intellect to justify it.

Why is this important? Because to get the most from your love, intimate, and sexual experience you need to understand there is a higher reason for the strong attraction. It goes beyond looks and a strong personality or the fact that she treats me nice. It's about how this person will help you evolve into the higher you and that generally involves some growth on your part. That's just the way it is. Now, does that mean the love should not be honored or that you shouldn't have a relationship with that person? Of course not. It just means you understand there's a deeper reason for why you all are together.

It took me a while to understand that with Bella even though I always knew there was a deeper lesson there. I could feel it the entire time I was with her. The fact I didn't have that lesson was part of the reason we persevered during the first few times we had very serious trouble in our relationship. But having that understanding allowed me to be in the love of our relationship, but not subject to it. It gave me the freedom to love her and love myself at the same time.

CHAPTER 12

A SADOMASOCHISTIC FRIEND INDEED

It could be said that the ability to transmute pain into pleasure is one of the greatest life tools one could ever have.

WHEN I WAS WITH the Tantric Goddess I choose to engage in certain sexual practices that scared me. These were experiences that I knew would be physically painful. I can't say why I decided to go to that place, but at the time I felt strongly about it. One thing I have always been keenly aware of throughout my sexual history is the differences in pain and pleasure thresholds between me and my partners.

What is the purpose of pain? Is there a Tantric lesson in masochism, which is the ability to derive pleasure from one's own pain? In my online travels I met a powerful warrior woman. Our connection was cool. I never physically met the sister, but she taught me a lot about the purpose of sex and what people's blockages are. For instance, many of my sexual experiences throughout life were filled with fear. I was scared shitless more times than I can remember when it came to sex. I wanted to perform well and please the woman I was with, but more than that I didn't want to look like an idiot. I didn't want to ejaculate early. I wanted to give the impression that I actually knew what I was doing, which in truth I didn't most of the time. I was pretty much copying what I saw on TV and in the movies and what my friends claimed to do in their experiences. There were only a handful of times in my life that I actually approached sex with mad confidence and those were times I was with a partner I had been with multiple times before or when I was extremely sexually active with a ton of partners in a short period of time. It's something about having sex with five or six different women per week over a two-year period that feeds your confidence like a motherfucker. The ability during those years to pull women of my choice into my sexual rotation with little to no effort says something about your sexual prowess and mastery. That said, I found these periods to run in stretches as opposed to being a permanent thing in my life. Other life factors enter the picture that tend to shoot down your confidence like moving to new places and having to relearn parts of the game or not being able to focus on the game for long stretches of time. If you don't use it you lose it.

How does the fear of failure affect us going into a sexual performance? Probably the same as it affects us in a musical performance or job interview. And for men who haven't had a lot of sex you really can't go into it nervous and fearful. From a man's standpoint you have to be sure of yourself and in control; otherwise, it's just a mess.

But what's inside of the pain – the illusion of the pain itself. The reality is you have total control over your experience and that the fear of pain had more power than the pain itself.

Initiate yourself my friend or be initiated.

Face your fears.

Enough said there, let's go back to the Tantric Goddess. When I was with her I remember her sucking on my chest and nipples during sex early in our relationship. I remember saying something to her about how it felt and me being sensitive on my nipples and somehow she received my communication as me liking hard, intense sucking in that area, teeth and all. In reality, I liked the opposite – a softer, gentler, more sensual approach to having my nipples stimulated. I remember after that she would suck on my nipples super hard and I would be like what in the holy hell is she trying to do besides bite these motherfuckers off? Dizzammm! Usually, I would say something off the bat, but I decided to go outside of my comfort zone. You see, The Tantric Goddess was a Scorpio so I had already adjusted my usual lovemaking style to be more intense, firm, and intrusive. Plus, I knew that she was playing an important role in my life at the time. I knew I was learning something from her so I didn't want to suppress her expression in any way even if it was uncomfortable for me. And this is not about her not being willing to change or adjust her style for me. She would have easily done whatever was in my best interest with no problem whatsoever. This was strictly a personal journey for me. It was me making a conscious decision to go outside of my comfort zone and have a new authentic experience.

Let me give some context here. When I say I'm sensitive on the nipples, I mean extremely. Like if the wind blows against them I'm trying to cover them up. Some of my girlfriends would play me like a video game just by steering my joints. When I say she was biting she wasn't nibbling on them gently. She was eating lunch in this piece. She might as well have slapped some hot sauce across my chest and pulled out a steak knife and fork. I mean it did hurt, but I never let her know. To be honest, I began to enjoy the pain and the fact that she enjoyed my reaction to her sucking.

I remember we were in the shower together washing each other when she turned around as was facing my chest. She was only about five feet three inches tall and was basically face to chest when standing in front of me. As she turned into me I remember tensing up because I knew what was coming. The other thing about being sensitive is how you react when those sensitive spots are stimulated in any way. It's like the more you react, squirm, cry, and wish they stopped, the more they dig in. It's like feeding off of energy. Men do the same thing when they hear women crying out in ecstasy during sex or when they think women are having an orgasm. It just makes you want to pound that nani harder than ever. When she turned into me, I looked down at her face, but she didn't look up at me. She stared at my right nipple. She seemed to go into a slight trance state or daze. All of a sudden she began to smile just a bit. It was a pretty scene with the water dripping down her face, her chocolate body sparkling against the light in the bathroom. I didn't resist. I grabbed the top of the shower door with both of my hands and squeezed tight. She put her left hand behind my back and her right hand on the side of my body – and then, my right nipple disappeared into her mouth. For the first ten seconds she was as gentle as the shower water dripping down her face. It was like she was learning my body all over again. Getting reacquainted with the texture and taste of my skin. Then a bite sent a sharp pain through my chest into my back and down my spine. My hands tensed up and squeezed more tightly to the shower door. Another bite followed just seconds after the first one and I began to wince with sounds that contained a harmonious mix of pain and pleasure. These would be the sounds that would feed her soul and provide her the reason to continue. She wanted to hear me again and again so the biting and intense sucking continued for what seemed like hours in the moment, but was only about twenty minutes in reality.

It's funny how the person bringing you so much pain can at the same time look so beautiful. It's funny how the water can feel so soothing at one point, but becomes so meaningless when you need it the most. When anything that soothes would be most welcomed and invited. She moved from my right nipple to my left. I turned towards her and leaned forward to make it easier for her almost like a human being voluntarily feeding a vampire who needs to blood in that moment. A part of me wanted to let go of the shower door and push her away from me so that the pain would stop, but I refused to let go. I refused to say anything to her other than express my pain and pleasure through moans. I allowed the rest of my body to move as it liked and it did. It twisted and turned trying to find a comfortable position or trying to move her teeth even a centimeter to the left or right. None of that worked. She was accustomed to my intense movements and squirming for comfort and stayed locked onto my chest like a suction cup. I learned to appreciate the shower water that night because it covered up the one or two tears that rolled from my eyes. I remember thinking how I was thankful for being in the shower as opposed to the bed. God is good.

I remember her pushing back off of my chest and examining her work. She stared at my red chest and swollen nipples as if she had just completed a beautiful piece of artwork. In her eyes was the same trance look she had before she started on my right nipple. She turned and got out of the shower, grabbed her towel and began drying herself off. I stayed in the shower for another five minutes just allowing myself to rebalance. I had to lean against the wall to ensure I wouldn't fall. My legs felt weak, my chest was sore, and my head felt light as if I had been shaken and stirred on the inside. But I was also happy that I had hung in there and not pulled my hands down and not pushed her away. I'm glad I allowed her to give me that gift. I remember feeling an overwhelming feeling of love and appreciation for her in those moments in the shower and afterwards. I thought about how beautiful she was, intelligent, and feminine. It's a wonderful thing to go beyond yourself in the care of those you love and respect and who love and respect you. I had the best night sleep ever that night. It was deep, peaceful, and without worry or thought.

The truth is I found great pleasure in those painful moments. It's like a rush or something and the intensity was unmatched. Maybe it's the same concept as bungee jumping or riding a rollercoaster or watching a scary movie. I know that I was able to use that lesson when I was pleasing women during sex. Even if what I was doing was uncomfortable or painful to me I was able to find the pleasure in it and focus on her. I've been able to use that in other parts of my life as well.

The Tantric Goddess never knew the pain and discomfort I felt when she sucked on my chest in that way. I remember her asking me one time if it hurt and I told her, "No." I didn't want her to stop, ever.

A SADOMASOCHISTIC FRIEND INDEED

CHAPTER 13

THE TIGHTEST PUSSY ON THE PLANET

Size truly does matter.

As men, we're going to encounter a number of different women throughout our lives, and this includes sexually too. The truth is most men won't know much about who a woman is sexually until we have sex with her and really even then we'll need a few sexual interactions with her before we really, really know. Even if you're a man who's waiting until marriage to have sex, it will be hard to be prepared for what your wife's sexual blueprint. Meaning, we won't know what her dominant sexual tendencies are and even more importantly, the specifics of her sexual physiology.

The basis and foundation of this book is sourced from the various sexual feminine blueprints I've encountered throughout my journey. It's this variation that's given me a great appreciation for the feminine as well as an understanding of my masculinity as well. Let's talk about tight pussy and the lessons therein.

As I've said, you can't predict the sexual physiology of a woman beyond the basic things like the size of her breasts, ass, and lips, which don't really tell you anything about her sexuality. Generally, these physical attributes won't define a woman's experiences and how she approaches sex. They will only have a slight impact on her current psychology when approaching sex; however, one physical attribute that will have a major impact on her sexual blueprint and psychology is the size, shape, and tightness of her vagina. Men need to understand that the size of a woman's vagina has a similar (not the same) psychological depth of meaning to her as does a man's penis size. Again, I'm in no way equating the two because rarely will a woman's chances with a man be ruined by rumors of her vagina being too tight or too loose. But it is something that will occupy her mind and it's also something she'll get feedback on from the men she has sex with. For example, a woman with a tight pussy may find that men ejaculate very quickly with her. If those men are insecure in their sexuality they may try to blame her for their poor performance rather than taking responsibility for their lack of sexual skills. The same goes for women with very wide vaginal openings where men claim to not really feel anything and sometimes claim they can't ejaculate. Again, these men are in need of sexual skills to assist them in having a fruitful sex life with a variety of women.

As a man, you shouldn't have any concerns about your penis size. I mean, none at all. Additionally, you shouldn't think that because you have a small penis or one that lacks girth that you won't encounter women with an extremely tight vaginal opening or tight vaginal walls. Men really need to understand the plethora and variety of women who are actually out here in the world. There are literally tens of thousands of women in every single shape and size that you can imagine. So change your mindset as a man and learn to attract the perfect partners for you as well as how mastering how to interact with all of these women.

Let me tell you a story. I've had two very specific and memorable experiences with women who had very tight pussies – Bella and Veronica. I've explained the impacts of Bella's tight pussy on me and the adjustments I had to make to simply enter her pussy, but to be honest, I never really mastered how to fuck that tight pussy in a way that would open her up to maximum pleasure even beyond the incredible feeling we enjoyed together. I didn't realize there was so much more that we could have done until I met Veronica.

When I met Veronica I was at a different stage of my life. I wasn't interested in being in love so much as cultivating very powerful connections with a variety of women who I felt had genuine love for me. That said, tight pussy has a way of pulling you in deeply to a woman. It demands your attention and focus and brings out your emotions in ways you may not be prepared for. Veronica was beautiful and thickly built. She was sweet and soft, but also had a hard edge about her, which I really liked because it made her truly independent in my eyes.

Veronica's pussy was extremely tight, but the first time we had sex, I didn't really experience the tightness because I entered her soft and I wasn't feeling my best that day. My overall vitality was low and I didn't have the energy to bring my sexual "A" game let alone get fully erect. The sex was still amazing though, and I really enjoyed being inside of her regardless. We wouldn't make love again for almost a year after that, at which time, I gained a full understanding for her tightness.

It's important to understand that a combination of tight and wet pussy during sex is an amazing experience to behold. It can change your eyesight. It can rewire the male brain. What separated Veronica's pussy from Bella's was the increased wetness of Veronica's pussy. It helped my penis slide into her a little easier and it allowed me to actually long-stroke her easier too. But that brings us to the point of the story – how do you work your penis inside of a tight pussy? How do you bring her maximum pleasure while also holding off your ejaculation? More importantly for me, was how do I continue to avoid causing my penis to become raw after continuous sex.

The first full weekend Veronica and I spent together, we had sex eleven times. It was raw, passionate, and intense. It surprised me actually because I became very animalistic with her and found myself almost out of my mind. That raw aspect of myself came to the forefront and attempted to consume every part of her. It was like I couldn't get enough. It wasn't just about the pussy, but also the strong feelings I had for her as well. I loved her and didn't hold back those feelings. Upon entering her, I had to go slow and slide my penis into her vagina at the right angle. There were times when I would have to pull back out upon first entry and start again, but I never had a worry of not getting inside of her.

Before I continue, let's define tight pussy. For me, tight pussy means there is a slight amount of pain upon entry into the vagina. It means I can't just slide right in the pussy, but instead always need to make a conscious effort to get inside. It means once I'm inside the pussy it feels like a hand grabbing my penis; especially, at the base of the shaft. It means fast pumping, at least initially, means causing her severe pain or discomfort. Tight pussy is tight to the tongue too, during oral sex. The opening of the vagina actually slightly grips the tongue. It means I can slide one finger inside of her, but two will take effort and will need consideration and caution. It means, you can't just yank your penis out of her without possibly stretching her or causing her to become swollen. In terms of swelling, I've noticed that tight pussy would always swell after multiple back-to-back sexual encounters even when done with care and little movement. Every women I've had sex with who's had a tight pussy has experienced swelling after multiple sexual encounters and this swelling would sometimes prevent us from having sex until it subsided. You'll also know her pussy is tight because she'll say that other men have commented on her pussy being tight. It will be a constant in her sexual life. That's tight pussy in my opinion. Remember, it's a ratio of penis girth to vaginal opening width that determines what penis has girth or which pussy is tight; thus, it's never a constant for most people. There are only a few who will find themselves consistently tight or with girth in all of their sexual interactions. Here's a formula for the technical folks out there:

Tight Pussy = Vaginal Opening Width/Penis Shaft Width

You can say vaginal opening is in centimeters and penis shaft width is either the circumference of the penis shaft or the radius of the penis shaft from center to exterior. As we can see it's completely subjective based on the participants.

Once I was inside of Veronica during the missionary sexual position, I made sure I stayed engaged with her. I kissed her deeply and looked into her eyes. I spoke of my love for her and stayed steady with whatever stroking I was doing in that moment. I found myself propping her legs on my arms just outside of my shoulders in order to allow the easiest and most friction-free stroking possible. The key focus and strategy is to slowly open her up and expand her. We need to understand that a vagina is a living breathing entity just like a penis and will expand and contract in order to facilitate the sexual experience, but it must be done in the correct way. It must be done with care and consciousness. Once I'm deep inside of her the deep kissing and looking into her eyes helps her relax. It takes some of the focus off the penis and pussy and puts it on the love we share. This is the key to helping to expand the vaginal opening to fully accept the girth of my penis. Short, grinding strokes inside of her pussy while I kiss her deeper and deeper and then slowly withdrawing my penis and expanding the length of the strokes. Eventually, I'm able to pull out of her where just the head of my penis is sitting at her opening and then slide it back in. For women with tight pussies, this technique is extremely stimulating. It's the longest stroke possible without completely withdrawing the penis out of the vagina. Once this physical state is reached, switching positions becomes possible and with less effort. It must be noted again that taking the proper amount of time and consideration is key to avoiding premature swelling of the pussy and to avoid rawness of the penis.

After that first weekend of intense lovemaking, I noticed

that my penis was raw and sore. This was due to my over-aggressiveness that weekend. That animalistic energy overtook me and caused me to stroke through the pain I may have felt, but wasn't quite in touch with. I remember being raw on our last night together, but still pushing through during our doggy-style sex session. I just wanted it so bad that I went beyond my physical limitations. That's an example of how not to engage a woman with a tight pussy because it leaves both partners in a state of needing time and healing. I wouldn't make that mistake again.

The vaginal opening is critical when assessing tightness, but what about inside the vagina itself? When I was with Veronica, I also felt all her vaginal walls literally pressing against and gripping my penis. This isn't always the case with tight pussy because sometimes once you get past the vaginal opening you enter into a more cavernous situation where there is little to no resistance or stimulation. In this instance it's important to work the walls.

I wanted to find her spots. Not just her g-spot, but all of the sensitive spots inside of her pussy and free the pain associated with those areas just like a massage therapist would do to your outer muscle. As I mentioned before, I would put her legs up on my arms, making sure I held them open and wide as a way to gain the most friction-free entry as possible. As I worked my way out of her pussy using the technique I described above, I began to work her walls. I started with her g-spot area by pushing her legs up higher and dropping my pelvis lower so that my erect penis was pointing upward to her top wall. I withdrew my penis, leaving only about an inch inside of her and began pushing upward and back to fully stimulate that top wall. This is where the maximum sensation was for her. This is where it is for most women. This is where she felt herself go deeper into her feeling place or orgasm and pleasure. It's a potential conscious blackout for her where she finds herself not only in intense pleasure, but going in and out of consciousness as she loses her bearings on where and who she is. I kept working the top wall, sliding my penis all the way back to cervix to ensure I've explored everything that top wall had to offer then I started working the side walls as well. Again, I used her legs as a way to help steer my erect penis. Shifting her raised legs to the left gave me access to her right wall. I shifted my pelvis to the left as well to give me more control. With her like all women, the side walls tend to be less sensitive at first, but after numerous sessions of the massaging, they begin to waken slowly. Also, massaging the side walls after intense top wall work will give her the opportunity to regain her bearings a bit. This will help her appreciate the pleasure and sensitivity she experienced with the top wall work.

To get to her bottom wall, I turned her around and put her in doggy-style position. I brought her to the edge of the bed and pulled her back every time she attempted to inch forward. I pushed her shoulders down into the mattress told her to put her arms straight out. This maximum arch looks good, but it's also necessary in order to reach the bottom wall within her. Bringing her legs and knees closer together helps to prop her up higher. I put my right foot on the bed right in front of her right leg and bent down to stroke her upwards. It didn't take me long to find sensitive points and friction on that bottom wall. One of the reasons why she must be eased open as discussed previously is because this stroking technique will put tremendous pressure on the top part of her vaginal opening; therefore, it's key that it be as soft and supple as possible before hitting the bottom wall. She found this position very stimulating, but it was also stimulating for me too as the bottom part of my shaft was being massaged. It took focus and concentration to stay steady without ejaculating prematurely in this position.

These techniques help to open her up and bring maximum pleasure to the lovemaking experience. The more we made love in this way, the more open her vagina was to my penis and the smoother our lovemaking became just like a hand and glove. The result is her pussy learning to grow and expand to accommodate a penis that has girth. The pussy can grow and expand and so can the penis.

THE TIGHTEST PUSSY ON THE PLANET

CHAPTER 14

SHAPESHIFTER

We are the builders, sculptors, and molders of our reality.

As MEN WE SPEND a good portion of our lives attempting to impress, date, and ultimately sleep with women. Let's be honest, our goal starting from an early age is to gain public acknowledgment and acceptance from a variety of women and of course the ultimate acknowledgment is drawers, panties, sex. We can't wait to tell the fellas about who we got with and where and how it all went down. Yeah, a lot of that is tied up in our inherited mommy issues as discussed in the "Mommy May I" chapter, but it's also about acceptance from our male peers. Then there's the whole puberty thing, which introduces the concept of pain and discomfort when carrying a nut sack full of reproductive fluid. Either way you look at it, it comes down to our ultimate desire of having sex with women.

One of the biggest challenges for us as men is we've ranked women based on looks and appearance; thus, putting ourselves in a bit of a quandary. Meaning, simply having sex with just any woman isn't going to cut it. She needs to be a woman who other men are impressed with and who'd they like to have sex with; otherwise, it's meaningless. Remember, this isn't about love or the pursuit of family, but our initial drive to connect with women, which is established based on childhood priorities and values. The challenge is we take these same values into adulthood as well and continue on that pattern of judging women based on the same appearance criteria we used as children.

The result is the women who like us don't get their interests reciprocated because they fall outside of our criteria for looks. This makes the available pool of women to choose from even smaller, creating increased competition among men and women, and increased frustration. Inevitably, you'll have a large pool of men who are left without options for women and an even larger pool of women in the same predicament. But wait, it gets worse. We also see a lot of men get into lying and leaving women out to dry after they've had sex because of the shame of their male peers knowing they had sex with an "undesirable" woman that no other man wants. Now women are being mistreated by men because of a childish value system and men are still left ultimately unsatisfied sexually and intimately. It's a major problem.

So how do we address this issue? I don't want to push men into accepting women they may not be attracted to as a standard for dating because that's not realistic, but I would like to offer a possible solution that's worked well for me. It's called the Female Choice Paradigm and explains why a woman might choose a man. It's essentially saying women have a heart centered and emotional mechanism that causes them to be drawn to certain men. It's not something that's really logical and when men observe this from the outside it may not make any sense. Maybe as a man you've seen a woman with a guy and wondered what in the hell she sees in him. You assume he must have money because there's no way a woman as fine as her would be with a guy like that. This is actually a common scenario where we see this kind of mismatch. You don't see it happening the other way a lot though where a super handsome man is with a woman who's subpar in the looks department. The latter scenario is way more rare.

Part of the explanation is the Female Choice Paradigm where her attraction is her attraction and it doesn't have to make any sense. Once a woman chooses a man, she sticks with him through thick and thin. It's an amazing phenomenon to observe, actually. We see men living with women and not contributing anything and she still accepts him. We see men cheating on women and the woman still accepts him. The list goes on and on. I'm not saying there are no cases where the issue with the woman is a lack of self-esteem, but that's only part of the reasoning. It's also the Female Choice Paradigm where something within her has selected this man and the connection is beyond logic, reason, or rationality. As men we'll never understand it because it doesn't work that way for us. When we select a woman, it's because she's providing some kind of direct value to our lives and when the drama from her exceeds the value, she gets cut off. Simple.

What I'm saying is that all men get chosen by women all throughout our lives. If we were to think about it, there are been so many times a woman has shown some interest in us and we've dissed her because she didn't look attractive. It's a quandary.

What I discovered is that when women choose me and I honor that choice by choosing them back and subsequently relating with them these women begin to transform and shapeshift. Meaning, they actually begin to look different than when I first started dating them. They become more and more beautiful the longer I'm with them. They've lost weight, tightened their bodies, and even went through facial transformations as well. Their process was conscious, but I'm arguing there's a metaphysical element to the physical and energetic transformative processes of women.

I realized that I'm a builder and shaper of my world and environment. I can take any woman who gives her heart to me and make her into my own image. This is a force within me that she can sense and is the foundation of her attraction to me; although she may not know it consciously. She knows I'm her healer. She knows I can bring out something within her that is currently dormant. I know I can make her better, healthier, more vibrant. I know I can bring out her goddess persona.

How do I do this? I do it through sex. I make love to her as if she is that woman in my vision. I make love to her knowing she is the dime I most desire. I don't make love to her as she is, but as she will be. I see her beauty now. I feel her tight body now. I toss her and flip her like I was making dinner in my personal alchemical kitchen. It's a conscious process.

I love when I'm with women who most men don't desire. I love increasing them to that universally desirable woman. As men we are builders, shapers, and alchemists. It's what we do and women are some of our greatest masterpieces.

It's true I stumbled upon some of these metaphysical skills by happenstance, but that's how all things come into the world – chance, accident, and through the unexpected. As men, we need to learn to bring out the beauty in our women because it's what we both desire. The key is to take her raw power, which is expressed through her intense attraction for us and use it to strengthen ourselves – the tool and chisel of our sculptures. Intense focus and dedication are what we utilize in the process. The force is felt through our lovemaking and physical molding of her body.

When I first came back in contact with Hanna I was pleasantly surprised how beautiful she still was. She had such beautiful eyes and such an innocent gaze about her, even though underneath all of that she was a powerful and very sexual woman. Her look and outward way can be deceiving. One of the things that stood out when we were in the hotel room was the additional weight she gained, which was a surprise to me because she seemed to naturally stay fit. Meaning, I never saw her exercise because that wasn't really her thing, but she stayed fit anyway. I always attributed her nice shape to her high sexual frequency. What stuck out most was her belly was chubbier than I would have expected. To be honest, it wasn't very attractive and kind of disappointing because it was so different than how she was the last time we were together. Her extra weight didn't get in the way of our lovemaking that weekend though. She was still just as sensual as ever. I put everything

I had into her and there was no doubt in her mind how much I wanted her.

Fast forward a few months later to when I'd see her again. This time, her shape was almost exactly how I remembered it from our time together years ago. I kept looking for the extra weight I had just experienced a few months before, but it was gone. I was genuinely surprised and even shocked by her slimmed down figure.

CHAPTER 15

THE GODDESS SEKHMET

Raise our masculine force in order to meet and acknowledge her feminine power.

THE GODDESS SEKHMET

It's always a challenge in relationships because we are always tasked with two things as men: (a) giving her what she wants and (b) giving her what she needs. Sometimes it can be a fine line to walk in deciding what it is she wants because she's not always going to say it and even when she does, it may not be accurate. We're all familiar with the concept of wanting something, but not being able to truly express what it is. The other side of the coin is whether what she wants is really the best thing for her at the time or at all. It can be disappointing to deny her what she really believes she desires for herself.

That brings us to the things she needs. The goddess Sekhmet is a powerful goddess with the energy and power of the lioness. She's fierce, direct, fearless, and beautifully sexy. Her magnetism makes the potential danger of interacting with her sexually well worth it even if you come out scathed as a result of the interaction.

All women fit into a general archetype persona. Feel free to use whatever system of archetypes you'd like, but the classification is helpful in understanding how to interact with them. The same applies to us as men. For example, we can be SOLDIERS, LEADERS, NEGOTIATORS, MONKS, PEACEKEEPERS, or a myriad of other archetypes that explains our dominant personality.

When I started dating Sekhmet, things started off slowly and smoothly. It was a long-distance relationship, but very lowkey. She was fierce and bold, but because she chose me, she was receptive to my authority and guidance. She was previously married and transitioning to being single. The longer we were together and the more stories she told me, the more I saw how her Sekhmet personality was revealed. She was a no-nonsense type of woman and would go toe to toe with her ex-husband on a number of issues. I wasn't interested in who was wrong or right during these confrontations, but rather how she handled herself and how her energy manifested in relationships.

Because she was so firm in who she was and what she wanted, it created an atmosphere of her always getting what she wanted with little to no resistance from those around her. I began to see how this played out in her life as she switched from job to job, entrepreneurial business to business. She did exactly what she wanted when she wanted, but it wasn't always the best thing for her long-term progress. Power is a beautiful thing, but it can't exist by itself and be beneficial in our lives; thus, the necessary interaction between the masculine and feminine.

As men, it can be hit or miss when attempting to exert your will inside of a relationship with a woman who's been married and had major challenges inside of her prior relationships. One minute she's taking your suggestions and being receptive to your guidance and the next she's rejecting it. This kind of fluctuation can go on for years inside of a relationship and is to be expected to be honest. We can't help but bring our past relationship experiences and fears into our new relationships. Reconditioning takes time and consistency.

There is one area where our will as men can be exerted and felt on the deepest level and that's during sex. As I stated previously with my experience with the Tantric Goddess, consistent, rhythmic lovemaking proved to be a valuable tool in helping her free herself from her mental limitations. In this case with Sekhmet, the steadiness of firm stroking is used as a reconditioning tool to provide an example of trust, structure, and consistency in her life. It's designed to show her what receptivity to the masculine can look and feel like and experience first hand the benefits.

Over the course of years, our sexual connection grew stronger and stronger. The sex became more and more pleasurable for both of us. The intensity of the orgasms increased and the joy of making love grew steadily. It was the kind of sex you think about, long for, and look forward to. Part of the quality that Sekhmet brings to the table is her desire for dominance, which may sound harsh, but isn't necessarily. Dominance can also manifest in the form of mastery where someone wants to see the deepest sides of you in order to know you fully and connect with you deeply. She expressed to me numerous times the desire to see my dark side. She knew it was there and wanted to experience it. I knew it was there as well and was open to her seeing it and experiencing it first hand; however, it was important that she first felt a force that equaled her perception of her power. There needed to be a mutual respect that went beyond ever her choosing me as a partner and even beyond her respect for my accomplishments. Feeling is the key here because Sekhmet is not an intellectual deity regardless of what she thinks. She has to see it, feel it, and experience it first hand in order to respect it.

As a man our body and mind is our tool. It's what we bring to the table to interact and influence those around us. We must keep it tuned, toned, and strong. Our minds must remain clear and steady. There is no bringing force to meet Sekhmet's power without having a legitimate physical body makeup that includes stamina, muscle mass, flexibility, and core strength. It's not about being cut up muscularly necessarily, but having a tool that's effective in helping us implement our will on earth.

With the Tantric Goddess, I was at my limit physically when providing her consistent, rhythmic lovemaking. I had to use my mind to compensate for what my body and fitness lacked. This can work and there will always be situations where the mind must compensate for the shortcomings of the body and vice-versa. But these should be exceptions to the rule because we want our bodies to be fit enough to support our work in all areas of our lives. In addition, the toll of going beyond your physical capabilities using your mind is high, meaning, we need to recover from overexertion of the body. It's not a sustainable way to live our lives and do our work. It's much better to strengthen the body to where our need to use the mind is minimized.

My lovemaking with Sekhmet was exceptional, but I was led to bring more force to our sessions in the form of consistency, rhythm, and firmness. I would also prepare her by having extended foreplay where she could relax into knowing that sexual intercourse wouldn't be rushed and that her maximum pleasure would be realized. In addition, foreplay for us would be extended where it could last for anywhere from thirty to forty-five minutes and wouldn't end until her orgasm was achieved on a multiple level. This to is a type of container that will rewire her to be more open and receptive.

As I entered her with my hard lingam, I made sure I kissed her deeply to increase our intimacy so she knows I love and care for her with all my heart. I wanted her to know that I loved eating her pussy and sucking her breasts and bringing her to multiple orgasms. I would stay kissing her passionately and keeping my lips connected to hers to further solidify our intimate connection. I would grind in her pussy with my lingam and shoot energy into her yoni as a way to stimulate her, but also as a display of my force; thus, letting her know I'm multi-dimensional in my lovemaking skills and that those skills will be respected by her and meeting her power head-on. This form of lovemaking can last for fifteen or more minutes, or as long as it needs too. We can switch positions as I see fit knowing that her orgasmic pleasure will be the result. It's both beautiful and connected lovemaking.

At some point, the work to give her what she needs must begin – the work to bring steadiness and consistency into her life. I find a position on top of her, with her legs in the air being held up on either side of my arms. Her feet are dangling to the side only eighteen inches from my ears. It's essential that her legs are held up high enough to tilt her ass and pelvis off the bed at an angle that allows me to fuck her dead into the center of her pussy with the least amount of resistance and friction. My hands must be firmly planted into the sheets and mattress such that they are comfortable yet strong. The best angle is as close as you can get to ninety degrees from the bed as possible with the weight of my shoulders shooting straight down into the mattress through my arms. The most critical piece for me was to ensure my head was almost directly above hers so that I'm looking down into her face and eyes. My eyes would act as the primary gate indicating that the only place she can go is within. The eyes don't lie. If a woman looks into your eyes and sees weakness, she's not going to have confidence in your or the process, which will make her uncomfortable and unable to find pleasure let alone go deep into herself. I take my time to find my rhythm making sure it's strong and fast enough for her to feel it deeply. It's got to be a firm, forceful pace, but it can't be too fast or hard like pornography or else it will trigger her mind to feel it's an abusive or selfish act, which is the opposite of what we want to achieve. Once the proper rhythm has been found, we must start without breaks, adjustments, or stoppages. We must hold our bodies still and locked. We must look into her eyes even when she turns away.

It's important to understand that she will turn away and Sekhmet did just that through our lovemaking. She would start with a look of uncertainty and disbelief as if this was going to be a temporary position that will be switched up soon enough. Even when she would start to go into trance and fade away, she would come back to see if this is really real and know whether she can trust the process. In all of those instances we are looking her dead in her eye in the same way I'm fucking her dead in her pussy. Over time, Sekhmet starts to fade and surrender because her normal outlet and experience is no longer available. Although she is Sekhmet, it's still a persona that sits on top of our essential self – spirit, soul, and consciousness. Once her persona fades the only thing left is ourselves in our essential state and the longer we stay in that state the more we get to know ourselves.

I rocked and pounded per pussy steadily. Just like with the Tantric Goddess, I was able to find myself as well. The rhythm not only puts her into trance, but allows me to go into a subtle trance myself. I am able to feel the God within me and see my alchemical abilities at work and that in and of itself is a transcendental experience.

I don't stop because I'm tired or uncomfortable, but because she has had a full trance experience and had the ability to travel to other worlds within my protection and care. At the end of the process, I kept my lingam inside of her and held her and kissed her deeply. It's important for me to stay connected to her and for her to know that I'm patient and present with her and not trying to focus on myself immediately after as if it was a strenuous process that I resented. I continued to hold her even when I pulled my lingam out of her.

This is how we rewire Sekhmet to know that she is protected and can trust your force to match her power. This is the work we as men must do to heal our women during sex. It's an unselfish act, but one that pays you and others dividend as well. Sekhmet is forever changed by this process, but also forever grateful.

PART II:
The Technical Details

CHAPTER 16

THE THIRTY-MINUTE ORGASM

THE CONCEPT OF A thirty-minute orgasm for a man is strange at best. Unbelievable and crazy at worst, but it's really not strange at all, especially now with a ton of "scientific" research to confirm something other than a five-to-ten second ejaculation for men actually exists. But I get it, thirty minutes? Come on. If that were true wouldn't I have seen one of these porno stars having one? Ah, no. Pornography is acting, not sex. These actors are too busy trying to entertain you to the point where they can't even really have sex. I know you think what they are doing is sex, but it's not. It's called acting and showmanship, which is all good, but it's still not sex.

The first hump (no pun) a man would need to get over is understanding he can have an orgasm as opposed to only an ejaculation. Is there a difference? Yes, and it's huge. Is one better than the other? Well, that depends on what your goals and preferences are in life. An argument can be made for both, but it's really comparing apples and oranges.

So all the men can relax because as you can see we are not talking about a thirty-minute ejaculation. Even though you probably wish I were talking about that. Can you imagine? Squirting for thirty-minutes straight. Actually, that may not be so nice. First of all, that's a lot of fluid loss. If a man ejaculated for thirty-minutes straight that's like bleeding to death. You would basically die of dehydration or malnutrition or something. Plus, that's a lot of wear and tear on the nut sack and penis shaft. The nut sack and prostate would have to produce volumes of semen at a rapid pace, which would probably overload them until they just broke down. Then you'd be shooting air nuts, which could be psychologically damaging. It's like having the dry heaves where you're throwing up but nothing is coming up but air and it feels like your body's trying to cough your nuts up through the throat chakra. That really sucks.

Let's understand what an orgasm is. You can look at the word and break it down into "organ" and "spasm" or into "organic" and "spasm." It's basically a naturally occurring and intense spasm in certain tissues and muscles in the body. It can be either localized like in a clitoral orgasm where the intensity is in only one part of the body, or widespread, covering multiple areas of the body simultaneously like a full-body orgasm. What causes the spasm? It's basically the stimulation of an area of the body with enough nerve endings to draw the mind all the way into that sensation. But more specifically, it's the intense energy flow through those tissues that is causing the rapid vibration and the groovy feelings.

An orgasm is a feminine expression of an intensely moving energy throughout the body. I say it's feminine because the energy stays internal and has no outward expression. If the energy were to express itself outwardly then it would be a masculine expression of energy. That's what an ejaculation is; a focused, controlled, and targeted release of energy with a specific aim and purpose. A purpose might be shooting semen into a hot wet vagina for the purpose of facilitating the growth of life.

In order for a man to experience orgasm he needs to put himself in a vulnerable feeling place. He has to allow himself to feel fully in any and all parts of his body wherever stimulation is felt. It requires complete vulnerability and openness. In order for a man to do this he must trust the woman he's with totally and completely, so if you feel ashamed or embarrassed to let your partner see you in ways you've never even seen yourself then you won't be able to experience the orgasm.

From there we can get into the meat and potatoes or at least the prerequisites to having an orgasm. It's the same direction needed for women and it requires them to be in their feminine nature.

The Devotee

There are two primary qualities to being a Devotee: one is being open and receptive to direction and the other is staying committed to it. Both of these qualities are female qualities and have historically been difficult for men. The only time a man is receptive is when it's from someone he has agreed to subject his will too. This is what you see in the military, intentional subordination to command. The receptivity we are referring to here doesn't discriminate. It's like the earth accepting whatever seed is sown. Commitment is a different story. It's the ability to stay the course regardless of other factors or outside influences. Again a feminine trait and one that can prove challenging to men. Men are wired to adjust to circumstance and honor contracts until the terms have been violated.

When it comes to achieving orgasm men need to learn to be receptive and committed. They must be receptive and accepting to the dictates of their feelings. They have to acknowledge their feelings. When you talk with Tantra teachers they will say that men often times miss out on most of the sexual experience because they are not in tuned with the subtle feelings taking place all over their body. What that means is most of the sensory inputs have been shut down. It's almost like someone poking you in the feet with a pin and you not being able to feel it because you are so focused on another area of your body.

This is a challenge for us in just living our lives. We don't embrace the "allness" of the moment and miss out on all that is being offered. And I understand fully that its human nature to avoid painful experiences and implement strategies to maximize pleasurable ones, but the secret to pleasure lies beyond the "pain." The more pain is avoided the greater its toll upon us, as it is now allowed to ravage the mind, body, and soul for eternity because we never get beyond it. We put it off until another time, but never stop thinking about it. The pleasure and high is in the unknown.

Orgasm is the ultimate submission process and submission requires trust, bravery, and a desire for the supernatural. For a man to achieve orgasm he has to submit to his feeling and subject his will and mind to his body. It may sound easy in word and description, but men are often focused on being in control and appearing strong to others. We often want things to go our way, which is the opposite of subjection; it's control and thus the difficulty with reaching orgasm.

The Conservationist

The Conservationist is a feminine principle that resides in all of us. It governs our ability to focus on only what matters; therefore leaving us with an abundance of energy to accomplish whatever we want in the world. We see this energy develop most strongly in elderly women, but we all have access to it.

The truth is an orgasm is a selfish thing. It's an all-about-me type of event. When women have orgasms it's all about them. The most a man gets when a woman orgasms is the psychological thrill of knowing he had something to do with her having that orgasm along with the entertainment of watching the facial expressions and cool seizure-like body movements she makes during the orgasm itself. The psychological thrill can be so great that it often times brings the man to orgasm as he tends to relax for a job well done and prepares to cash in on the prize – ejaculation! Eureka!

As a note, there are actually other benefits to the man of a woman having an orgasm that are outside of the context of this book.

When we're in our masculine nature as men we're not so much worried about our ejaculation during sex. In life there are two things that are always guaranteed for men: death and ejaculation. So we really have nothing to worry about most times we have sex. When I say ejaculation is guaranteed I'm speaking about a majority of men, as I do realize there are some men who have issues ejaculating due to psychologically induced traumas from earlier in their life. As a result, we can focus on our partner and ensuring that she is fully taken care of as her orgasm tends to be more of a crapshoot depending on her training and openness. So the complimentary masculine trait practiced during sex is selflessness.

Conversely, the feminine trait practiced during sex is selfishness. I know that sounds fucked up to say, but it's the truth and there's absolutely nothing wrong with it. I'm not saying women have to be totally selfish throughout the entire sexual process and that rarely happens; however, if you plan on having an orgasm as a woman you need to be selfish. And guess what, the same holds true for men. Now any woman reading this is like, men are already selfish during sex. They ejaculate immediately or don't take their time and ensure the woman is engaged. Men are not innately selfish during sex, but they are largely inexperienced and lack confidence and training and therefore aren't in their masculine and often ineffective. That said, if a man wants to experience an orgasm he needs to learn to be selfish.

Selfishness means that you take the time to honor everything you feel during sex. It means that when you feel something you allow yourself to enjoy it and let it move you in any way that it chooses too. That's excruciatingly hard for men to do. We're used to controlling situations and denying ourselves the opportunity to feel most of the sensations that come up during sex. We're thinking about baseball or anything that will prolong ejaculation. That's our training in everything in life. We learn in sports to play through the pain; ignore it. If you don't then you're a punk or a sissy. Result? Desensitization. Is it a bad thing? Nah. It's important to learn to go beyond your sensory body. That was my self-taught lesson in the chapter *A Sadomasochistic Friend In Deed*. To learn the pain is really just a signal and interpretation by the brain as opposed to something real in and of itself.

An orgasm is a full-body experience. It's a "gasm." Just picture what a "gasm" looks like. It's spastic and seizure-like in nature – a vibration uncontrolled. Imagine what it feels like when your entire body is shaking uncontrollably or spazzing out, so to speak. It's pretty nice actually.

So step one is learning to feel again and not sidestepping any part of the sexual experience. For example, when I was with Bella I rediscovered what it felt like for the head of my penis to hit the entrance of some tight wet pussy. It was awesome, orgasmic in fact! When I first started having sex as a youngling I was more focused on just getting my joint up into the pussy as fast as I could so I could start pumping one hundred miles per hour. But on the real, I realized how good it feels to just hit the entrance of pussy. I remember feeling that before back in the day, but I had to cut it off or else risk ejaculation and a bad rep. There were other things I rediscovered about sex when I opened myself up to feel like how my balls felt sitting square in the crack of an ass while in the missionary position or a woman's soft touch on your chest with her hands. I remember when I was with the Tantric Goddess rediscovering how emotional I would get just looking into her face during love making. It was such a great feeling to see that; it would touch me to my soul. How about the softness of a woman's feet against your torso, neck, and face or the smoothness and softness of her waist when making love to her from the back. There were so many good things I rediscovered during my sexual journey all of which helped me achieve massive, extended orgasms.

The challenge for men will be to discover these treasures once again and feel them in their fullness. Appreciate everything being offered during the sexual experience. Will you ejaculate if you do this? Surprisingly, the answer is no. Why? Because you are releasing all the thoughts, emotions, and feelings all while feeling a high level of pleasure making the desire to ejaculate almost zero. In addition, because you are releasing tension and stress you will feel more balanced during sex, avoiding any build up of energy and thus a desire to release that energy, ala ejaculation.

We have to understand that ejaculation occurs due to a build up of energy in the body. It's one of the ways we detoxify our system because we are not just physical beings, we are energetic beings as well. That's why you "feel" relaxed after ejaculation because you released the excess energy from the body, which restores it to a normal, balanced vibration.

The Lover

This may seem like a silly question, but do you know how to experience pleasure? Maybe a better question is do you really want to experience pleasure? The truth is, most of us don't. We actually hold our pleasure hostage to a limited set of stimuli like certain shapes of women, warm weather vacation spots, raspberry cheesecake, the weekend, days off from work, lunch time, summer vacation, Jim Carrey comedy movies or that special sitcom on television. That may seem normal, but the truth is it's not normal. As human beings we have the ability to be joyful at the drop of a dime or experience pleasure wherever, whenever, and with whomever. That's what freedom is. It's the ability to express yourself in any way you want to without seeking permission from others or needing specific situations or material objects to initiate or justify that feeling.

When we look at our metaphysical makeup, there's a part of us that loves just because. The Lover in us loves pleasure, people, relating, and life overall. As a result *she* doesn't discriminate in what she enjoys and therefore lives each and every moment to the fullest. You've seen those people, right? They're always happy, smiling, and in a good mood. It can make you sick to your stomach sometimes and you want them to have a bad day every once in a while like the rest of us. Well, we do at least until they have a bad day, then we feel like crap because the one consistent ray of light in your life has gone out and you miss their positivity and lightness even if only for a day.

To take on the attributes of the Lover we must get lighter. We must learn to appreciate life, people, and opportunities and not hold on to our prejudices and angers. So as a man seeking his orgasmic nature it's required that he appreciate and love the woman he is with as well as each sexual experience they have together. Cherish it, honor it, and look forward to it. This will be true for any woman he chooses to be with which makes plenty of sense when you think about it. I mean, why be with someone you don't cherish and love? Why take the time and share your body, mind, and soul with them? And while you're there, why not enjoy the entire process to fullest without glossing over any parts? Feel every nook and cranny, so to speak.

Tying It All Together

If you are able to pull these attributes together then you'll be well on your way to achieving orgasms during sex. Incidentally, these are the same steps women should follow as well and it should be easier for women as many of these character attributes will come more naturally to you. I know some men are reading this and saying these instructions sound too easy and generic to generate a thirty-minute orgasm, but the truth is, for men, these instructions are not easy. As men we just haven't learned to be vulnerable with our feelings and emotions. We don't cry in public, say we're hurt, or tell our woman how much we absolutely love her pussy right there in the moment. This, my friend, is the doorway to a whole new level of pleasure.

So, once you start doing this work, will you achieve a thirty-minute orgasm? No. But you will achieve a thirty-second orgasm and the more you stay open and vulnerable the length of your orgasm will continue to increase until one day you'll look up and say, "I just had a thirty-minute orgasm."

CHAPTER 17

HOLDING THE SEED

WHEN I WAS IN involved in spiritual culture the concept of "holding the seed" or not ejaculating during sex was a big thing amongst the men in the community. It was seen as a path to power and enlightenment if it could be done over a long period of time.

However, there's a misconception that men, holding back their ejaculation, is actually pleasurable during sex. This is actually not true other than the feelings of accomplishment during the act. The beneficial feeling of not ejaculating for a man during sex comes after the sex act and usually lasts for at least twenty-four hours. That feeling is not one of pleasure, but power. Anyone who has every consciously held their semen *properly* during sexual intercourse knows there is no special pleasurable feeling resulting from that experience. The sex still feels good, but that's the extent of it. I say properly because benefitting from holding back an ejaculation requires more than just holding back the ejaculation. It requires that it be done at the right time during sex, not to soon and not too late.

The power results from a build up of what Master Sunyata Saraswati calls the prana shakti or energy that is responsible for propelling the semen out of the shaft of the penis. As you approach ejaculation this energy builds up inside the body, but if you don't ejaculate and don't get too close to ejaculation this energy is available for use in other ways in the body. The other ways the energy is used is dictated by the body's indwelling intelligence and could go towards healing, balancing, or support of any number of functions. But whatever it is the body decides to use this energy for you will definitely feel it. It almost feels like a fountain of youth and the good news is there will be more energy left over for you to use as you please as well. You can also direct this energy to various parts of the body, but that's a separate topic.

Have you ever done something to improve your health, like taken a potent vitamin, herb, remedy, massage, acupuncture, drink fresh squeezed juice, etc., and felt a huge energy boost from it the next day, even though you may not have been aware the energy boost was from your previous day's actions? Most of the time you just use that energy by doubling the amount of work you get done before you even realize that you had the extra energy. It's usually after the fact that you realize you had extra energy that day. Well that's what a power and energy boost feels like when you hold in your semen from sex. You just have more of it. You become a more powerful, more aware person on the planet in that instant. That's the whole concept behind sexual alchemy. It's the study of how to transmute energy generated through the act of sex into power to be wielded at man's will. We want the ability to generate energy at will to be used as we see fit, but in order to do that we need to evolve past a purely sensual gratification of sex. We have to think beyond ejaculating or getting a piece and move towards generating the power to achieve our goals on the planet.

There is also a misconception that the male orgasm, not ejaculation, has something to do with holding the semen and waiting until just before ejaculation and pulling the energy up the spine into the base of the brain and that action has some sort of intense pleasurable effect during sex. This isn't true. The male orgasm has nothing to do with holding anything or any form of control by the male. The male orgasm is a releasing of the will in order to experience the energetic connection with someone in the moment. It's a releasing and surrender and has nothing to do with control. That said, a man can wait until he is about to ejaculate and refrain through breathing exercises and other techniques. At times during that process a man may feel a slight elevated feeling of pleasure, but this is not an orgasm. Also, the man may feel a sense of accomplishment for holding back his ejaculation, but again this is not an orgasm. Again, you'll have to try this for yourself to know.

A man has an orgasm, not ejaculation, the same way a woman does, by releasing and letting go. The orgasm is achieved by experiencing the pleasure and feeling of connecting intimately with his partner in the moment without judgment, filters, or thinking. It's an experience to behold as opposed to a process to control.

Sustenance Technique

So how do you have long-lasting sexual intercourse without ejaculating too early or not at all? Is there an ancient Buddhist technique that's been passed down for thousands of years? Or maybe there's a secret elixir made up of a mix of horny goat weed, yohimbe, and black cohosh? One shot of it will keep your cock hard for a month allowing you an average of twenty ejaculations per day. Actually, what I really heard is that a few years ago the government recovered a secret cock hardening technology from an alien crash site. First it was used to harden tooth enamel, but renowned scientist George Vandurburennn found it out through a freak accident (wink) that it could be applied to a man's erect penis keeping him erect for a three year time period.

Okay, okay, it's none of those things. I mean I'm sure there are some ancient techniques that can be applied and we know there are some herbs out there that can do the trick. Horny goat weed is a primary ingredient in certain prescription erectile dysfunction medications. But apart from these things, I would like to think we have everything we need help our sex life be great and give us more control over when and how we ejaculate during intercourse. To me the key is in our ability to be within and channel our masculine nature.

There are four primary masculine natures that each man should aspire to when looking to have the greatest impact in his relationship, career, and sexual life. Each of these masculine natures was covered in detail in my book *Tame Your Woman: How to Become the Man She Needs*. These masculine natures are the Monk, Leader, Soldier, and Negotiator. I'm saying that it's your swagger and mindset that has the biggest impact on your sexual performance and erectile longevity. These are more important than any technique; not that techniques aren't important because they are. But how can you perform or execute a sexual technique if you lack the basic elements of manhood? You really can't even if you get results that in your mind you would consider successful. Let's see how these masculine natures can help us with sex.

The Monk: Knowing is Half the Battle

Your Monk nature governs knowledge, wisdom, and understanding as well as your desire to set direction and objectives in your life. So we see what the first issue is already with most men when it comes to sex. They have no idea what sex really is or what its true purpose or potential is. I know that may sound silly to a number of men; especially, when the ego is on full blast. But what is sex for? Procreation? Getting your rocks off? I'm serious here. Stress relief? If sex is for any of those reasons then longevity is not required and obviously the penis and vagina would be constructed to promote expedient ejaculation. How can you be good at something when you don't understand the purpose of it? Most of our knowledge around sex is from pornographic and romance movies, soap operas, and the invaluable knowledge of our friends from high school on. Next would be a series of trial and error sessions with our many sexual partners.

Sex is the act of connecting physically and energetically with your partner on the deepest level we're capable of. It's becoming one with them consciously so that we may truly know them and our potential as unified beings. That's what sex is. The purpose of sex is for healing and manifestation or creation. Healing meaning each partner leaves stronger than before they engaged in sex and manifestation means you are building a new reality together to further your goals on the planet. You're literally combining your power with another to energize a collective reality. If you don't know you're connecting with someone's energy, you might try to fuck them every time, and not realize a softer approach and gentleness may be required to actually make that connection valuable. If you don't know you have the power and responsibility to heal, then you may harm the one you're with. There's a thin line between healing and hurting. Not only that, but you can't heal someone in three minutes. You're going to need some time; like hours, to really heal one another and that's great news because if sex is for healing and healing takes hours then we must be built to have sex for hours.

Understanding you are initiating a connection with your partner affects your mindset going into the act itself. It changes how I approach her, how I touch her, if I touch her, etc. I may not put my dick inside her pussy for an hour or so into our lovemaking. Although I planned on fucking tonight maybe I realize that that's not even what's needed. Maybe she needs some full body massage work followed up with repeated orgasms as stimulated by a g-spot massage with your hands. You need to have a goal for the session before you go into it else you leave it to chance and we don't want that do we? When I have sex with my wife I know what the goal is going in. I know if she is stressed and needs penis penetration or energy work or clitoral massage or just talking to her all night until she falls asleep.

More important than having a plan going in is having an understanding of all the tools and the landscape. I mean we're talking wisdom, knowledge, and understanding here. Do you understand the female body and how it works? What makes it tick and how to bring it to life? Better yet, do you understand your body and what makes it tick? Do you understand how to touch a woman and where to touch her? What's the best method for performing oral sex and when? Which intercourse positions stimulate a woman's g-spot versus the deep spot? Do you understand the proper way to perform friction sex (which is what you see in the porno movies) versus energetic sex, which is more tantric in nature? Can you bring a woman to orgasm on the phone with just your words and energy and can you bring her to an energetic plateau without touching her when she's in your presence? This is what I mean. How are you going to approach sex and have success without understanding the landscape? You have to know these things and when to apply them and how; otherwise, you become one-dimensional and ineffective. This lack of knowledge will also limit your plans and expectations. You can never approach a situation the same every time. Life is not built that way and believe me, neither are women. By nature and design, women are the most complex creations in the universe so you need to have some understanding going in when dealing with them on any level; especially sexually.

Another part of being a Monk is following your intuition. Intuition is the process of concluding a truth with surety without logical or analytical processing. If while making love you intuit what needs to be done to make the lovemaking more enjoyable or beneficial for your partner, then you should follow it. Following your intuition is one of the most important things a man should learn to do. Having a strong intuition is like being connected to God or an Oracle at all times in real time. It's free, real time truth delivered instantly to your dome. All you have to do to strengthen your intuition is follow it and it will get stronger within you. So if your intuition tells you to stop pumping at eighty miles per hour inside the vagina and instead sit still with half your penis in her, you should do it. It may save your marriage and I'm not exaggerating in the least.

I'm just scratching the surface here, but take my advice, put yourself on a continuing sex education curriculum from any source you see fit. It will pay off in the long run and you'll feel more confident going into sex because you'll actually know what you're doing. Most men ejaculate early during sex because they are nervous and stressed out. Why? Because they are clueless about what they're doing and have a strong suspicion they're going to fuck shit up by the time the sex is over. That's no way to be. Remember taking a test in school and you knew you were prepared ahead of time? You went into that bad boy relaxed, smiling, laughing, chilling. That's what it's all about. When you didn't study you had to wear extra deodorant because the stress level would be so high. You would get half the answers wrong because you'd be too nervous to even think and the other half because you weren't prepared. So get your Monk straight my friend. It builds trust in you; thus, self-confidence is assured.

Leadership

As I said in Tame Your Woman, leadership is one of the most misunderstood character traits on the planet. In the Monk section I described the importance of knowledge and understanding. By the time you get into your Monk personality you begin to acquire a plethora of information and tools to use when making love to your woman. But how do I know what tools to use and when once you're in the mix? That's where your Leader comes in. It's your leadership nature that understands when in real time to apply certain tools and techniques because only the Leader can see things for what they truly are. Only the Leader is truly present in the NOW. The Monk doesn't know when he will have to apply his knowledge, but he has it. The Leader is the one that knows when it should be used because the Leader can see clearly the situation at hand. It's the Leader within you that understands how your wife is feeling, what mood she's in, how she's responding to oral sex, massage, g-spot stimulation, and kissing, and as a result knows when to keep going, change directions, or stop altogether. This is important.

When you talk with women one of their other desires is a man who is present with them and is tuned into their ever-changing moods and desires. You have to be like that as a man, especially during sex. But it's not just about her. It's about you too. You have to be present with yourself and know when you're getting to the point of getting ready to ejaculate and have the presence of mind to stop or change something before you go over the edge. You have to know what strokes are extra-sensitive to you with the particular woman you're with. Why keep doing something that you know is going to lead to ejaculation? What's the point of that? Take control and be a Leader in the bed. Don't drive the car off the cliff. I mentioned earlier that you need to be in touch with what she wants and desires during sex and you might find a position, stroke, or pace that she really loves, but if it's going to make you cum then find something else. I don't care if she's upset or not. She'll really be upset if you ejaculate ten minutes into intercourse so get your priorities straight.

Let me reiterate what I'm saying. You have to be in control of your interaction with your partner. If not then you're not in control and that's when ejaculation can come at any time and when I say control I mean total control. If you need to pull your dick out of the pussy and get fifteen minutes worth of head then so be it. And we're not asking here; we're telling. If a woman is having sex with you it means she's giving you the reigns. She wants you to bring her to the Promised Land. The exception is if she's in the masculine role and you're in the feminine in which case you can put the book down now or give it to her so she can steer your ass to where she wants to take you. But that's a good point while I'm on it. If you don't take control during sex then she will. It's in a woman's nature to fill the void in her life. If no man steps up in her life she will step up her damn self. And it's not because she wants to step up and take over it's because she feels she must because there's a void there and if she does step up she'll resent you for it no matter what she says to you.

How does a woman know you're in control and present and accountable? Eye contact. As a man you have to look your woman in the eye during lovemaking. She needs to not only feel, but also see the confidence in you and looking in the eyes is the best indication of whether or not you're in tune with what's going on with her and you. If she sees you are comfortable and confident through this eye contact then she will relax and follow. If you look scared, worried or confused, or your eyes are closed, she'll begin to assume control of the ship. That's just the way it goes and when this happens during sex it screws things up royally.

This control thing is one of the biggest issues in relationships, not just with sex. Men are too comfortable with letting women lead in the bedroom and everywhere else for that matter. Ya'll need to cut that shit out before your testicles atrophy and just dissolve into fairy dust particles. I hear guys say it all the time, *"She wanted to be in charge so I just let her."* What the fuck are you talking about? Go back downtown and reapply for your man card and get back into the driver's seat Holmes. That's if you want to work on becoming a man, which is not mandatory by the way. Yeah, she's going to challenge you. That's in a woman's nature and thank heavens that she let's you know your leadership is lacking before someone outside the house does and it costs the family thousands of dollars or something equally damaging.

And I really mean it; you don't have to do these things. You don't have to be the Leader of your household. I'm simply giving some information to help maximize your sexual experience, but these are not hard and fast rules. But for those who choose this path step up your Leadership nature. Feel the power, rush, and confidence of taking control and responsibility for your situation. It's empowering and freeing. Be patient with yourself if this is new for you. It will come in time.

Soldier

Think about if your Monk and Leader are in order. What does that translate into? Fearlessness! What is there to worry about if you're armed with knowledge, presence, and a take-charge attitude? Only fear itself, my friend. A Soldier is about fearlessness and putting in work, which is what you need to be about when approaching sex with your partner. You can't go into sex worrying about the worst-case scenario. That's a train wreck waiting to happen. You have to just execute and if you've done the Monk and Leader work then you'll be ready to execute with no problem.

But wait…let me bring this closer to home. Too many men are actually scared of the pussy. You're nervous and even after twenty plus odd years of fucking you're still second-guessing yourself in the sizack (bed). Women can smell fear just like cologne and it dries them up like prunes. When women smell fear they get nervous themselves and start to panic and prepare plans to abandon ship or worse yet, take it over. You may think I'm stretching the truth here, but what I'm saying is true. If you're not a fearless man you won't make your woman wet. You'll have to rely on baby oil and oral sex to get her pussy wet. Why do women love thugs? It's because they have cojones. It's because they're fearless. Thugs don't care about other people's feelings, the law, the consequences of their actions, but most of all their own safety or future and although this may not be smart, you can best believe it's sexy as a motherfucker and women open their legs wider than a mother to gets some of that. They'll tell you they're hanging with their girls to get some of that. They drive around the corner on their lunch break to gets some of that there.

Do you understand the raw adrenaline rush of fearlessness, of moving with surety of foot? It feels better than sex. It feels better than getting slow, wet, sloppy head in your family room wearing flip flops, a wife beater, and boxer draws on a Sunday afternoon in the fall, while you're watching the football game with a slice of pizza in one hand, a beer in the other, and your team is up by twenty-one points – and I'm off tomorrow and the rent is paid for this month and next. Is that good enough for your ass? Sex becomes the icing on the cake compared to the hormone rush of fearlessly dominating another person or situation. That's why the warrior in the movie always kills his enemy even when his enemy is on the ground hurt and defenseless quibbling in fear. It just feels good. This fool begging for his life is making my dick hard. I've got to finish him and bust this nut off. I'll wipe my dick off on his shirtsleeve. That's some old baller shit right there.

FINDING MALE SEXUALITY

The prerequisite for becoming a Soldier is to get your Monk and Leader in order. In the beginning of your journey it will help to know a thing or two (Monk) and have an appreciation of when to apply that knowledge (Leader). That will help you move with some confidence and without excess thought or worry. Think about the war movies or the ones that have thousands of warriors with swords charging their enemy. Believe me when I say these motherfuckers aren't thinking about much except running as fast as they can toward the enemy lines to start slitting ninjas. The general or leader does all the talking and all the thinking. He gives the pep talk and warrior speech in the beginning for the sole purpose of suspending your thought processing. When you hear a call to arms speech the general is addressing all your concerns, all your fears. He's saying shit like,

> *"I know you are scared. Many of you have families, children, and a career to get too. Trust me I know all to well. But believe me men; if these bastards cross our borders all our families are dead, if they're lucky. Your wives will be sex slaves for their entire battalion for months before they're tortured and killed. Your kids will be killed on the spot and everything you've worked for will be for naught. Do you want that to happen? Do you?! If you're with me let's get these sons of bitches and protect what is rightfully ours! AHHHH!!!"*

You get the picture. That will get a motherfucker worked up in a hurry. There's nothing else to think about except for fifty men gangbanging your wife and daughter. Ahhhhh!!!! Charge! How is that for courage? Well, maybe not courage, but rage, blind rage at that. You get the picture.

Another aspect of being a Soldier and being fearless is being in shape. You can't be fearless and be out of breath. I'm not sure if you've noticed, but courageous folks have a lot of energy. They're running after motherfuckers on the battlefield and appear to be tireless. The last thing these guys are thinking about is a nap or a sandwich or cup of juice. Not being in shape during sex will fuck with your mind. You'll start thinking about how to get some rest and your woman is waiting for you to kick it in overdrive to knock down a series of eight to ten orgasms. That's a conflict of interest and it fucks with your confidence. Being out of shape in the bedroom is like fighting the king black dragon with your hands tied behind your back. You're basically a walking chicken nugget in that piece.

While I'm on this topic let me shed some additional light on why these masculine natures aid in your staying power during sex. One of the main issues with men cumming too quickly during sex is stress and lack of willpower. One of the ways we can fight stress is by being in shape or synthesizing oxygen. Your brain feeds off of oxygen, but if it can't get any then you can't think and problem solve. Just food for thought.

Negotiator

I can't begin to explain how important it is to talk to a woman during sex. You can actually put a woman at ease and into a state of trance just through talking to her and when she's relaxed she'll become wetter and more receptive, which puts less pressure on you to make something happen. Instead, you can work with her and create together.

Following our masculine nature path thus far, we have wisdom with the Monk, control with the Leader, and fearlessness with the

Soldier. I don't know about you, but if I have all of that in order, you best believe I'll be speaking my mind in the bedroom.

"Girl slow it down. Now grind deep and hard until you feel my cock massaging your cervix. Slowly. Slowly. Okay, now grind on it. Good. Grind harder. Yes! Now stay steady just like that while I works mine."

See how that works? It's easy to speak when you got your other shit in order and you're speaking with such confidence that she's going to believe and follow every word you say. How could she not? That's when you go from asking to ordering and from wishing to knowing. It's a nice feeling. My warning though is you need to have all four of these masculine natures in order for best effectiveness. I often times see men putting their Negotiator out there and doing a lot of talking, but lack knowledge or fearlessness and look like fools or get their bluff called and lose all credibility in the bedroom and streets.

What's even bigger than your partner responding to what you are telling her is you yourself responding. The more you talk with confidence the more you both believe what you're saying. So if you are saying, *"Girl, I'm gonna fuck you all night long with this big rock hard cock!"* What happens? Your brain starts believing it too and before you know it your body makes all the physiological shifts necessary to allow you to fuck for ten hours. This is not an unusual phenomenon. We've all talked ourselves into going beyond our perceived limits. It's just a matter of us believing in ourselves, which is why I say to have your Monk, Leader, and Soldier in order before you start the talking.

HOLDING THE SEED

CHAPTER 18

MEASURING MALE SEXUAL VITALITY

FIRST OF ALL, IT'S important to realize that self-evaluation in various areas of our life is important. We all need the ability to look at ourselves and see if we measure up to either our potential or whatever is required for success. The question then becomes, what's required for success? For each man it will be the standard of his choosing. For example in the area of sexuality I choose to measure myself against the optimal male in his prime as well as against a guru or Taoist master who has cultivated his sexual energy. What I mean is I shoot for my potential and not just the norm. I do this for everything whether it's health, fitness, mental acuity, or fatherhood because I want an accurate standard regardless of how I may be measuring up at the time. It's better to know than not to know.

There are certain ways men can evaluate their sexual health. It involves some very obvious and some not so obvious factors. Let's start with the basics.

Your Penis

Your penis is one of the best measures of your sexual health. When your body is not healthy enough to have sex or procreate your penis won't work. It's that simple. It's not that there's something wrong with your penis per se, it's that your reproductive system is shut down due to an overall lack of energy and vitality.

The penis is an energy-based organ; meaning, it only works when there exists a minimal amount of energy in the body that is able to flow to it. If the energy is there and is able to flow into the penis then blood will follow filling up the vacuum of space created by the energy expansion. We need to understand that we are both physical and energy bodies, not just physical. A physical body by itself is inanimate. It takes energy to give it life and fuel its functioning and although energy is neither created nor destroyed, according to physics, and is therefore infinitely abundant, there are no guarantees it will be abundant within our bodies forever. As a matter of fact, it won't, which is why we ultimately die. We die because we lose our ability to hold, recycle, gather, and utilize energy. As the energy leaves our bodies we notice signs of decay and deterioration like gray hair, impotence, cancer, fatigue, infertility, senility, and the host of other ailments and diseases classified by the medical establishment.

I also have to mention that along with energy loss as a primary reason for death and disease there is energy blockage which prevents the flow of energy to certain organs and parts of the body; therefore, literally starving them to death. This is also a contributing factor to things like organ failure or in the case of the penis, erectile dysfunction.

The challenge is how to identify these energy deficiencies before they become debilitating, irreversible conditions. For the purposes of this book and its subject matter lets determine signs of energy loss related to our sexual vitality as men.

Let's Discuss Size

As boys and men, we go through so much mental tension around the size of our penis. Some of our deepest mother acceptance and pleasing issues come to the forefront around penis size. First of all, no man should feel badly about his penis size because all penises are effective when it comes to giving women deep orgasms and pleasure. That's the truth. I've talked to numerous women who've admitted that some of their best sexual experiences have been with men with small penises. I know as men are reading this, they still don't feel any better if they in fact have a small penis. This is super deep for us and I totally get it.

There are some additional reasons why men shouldn't feel self conscious about the size of their penis; mainly, the fact they can change it. I know this to be true through my own personal experiences as well as other men and women I've talked too. This chapter is about how men can grow their penises.

The first time I heard about penis growth was when I was in high school. This girl I knew, who I was attracted to because of how open she was sexually, came to me one day and asked about her boyfriend. The conversation went something like this:

Barbara: "I'm not sure what to do. My boyfriend Michael's penis is really small and the sex isn't that great because of it. I'm having a hard time feeling him. What do you think I should do?"

I didn't know what to tell her. I'd never been asked anything like that, plus, I wasn't getting any pussy my damn self, so I had no context. I wanted to fuck her really bad myself, so I was at a loss.

But here's what I was thinking – Barbara was known for being sexually promiscuous at a young age, which at the time was looked down upon. Unfortunately, our culture looks down upon sexuality in general; thus the need for this book, but especially women's expression of sexuality. The promiscuous girls in my school were talked about and often times teased, but Barbara didn't care. I admired her for that. All that said, I figured that her boyfriend Michael's penis wasn't too small, but her pussy was too wide from all the sex she was having. That was my honest first thought.

A few weeks later Barbara approached me again and said not to worry about the question she raised before because his penis grew. I was like, "What the fuck?!" I couldn't figure out how his penis grew. She eluded to the fact that the more they had sex, the bigger it got. That was my first exposure to the concept of penis growth. But that example isn't only about penis expansion, but vaginal tightening as well. The point is sexual organs grow and shrink to support what they need to be. If you're with a partner who's got a big pussy, your penis can expand to accommodate the size difference.

As I got older and more experienced with sex, I was able to delve deeper into this concept. I was able to apply some of my sexual alchemy principles to penis growth. I was also able to observe many of my partners doing the work to tighten their pussies and saw it working beautifully. They were using yoni eggs, doing kegel exercises, and more to tighten their pussies and give it that snapback effect. So what about the men? There are plenty of exercises to help men hold their ejaculation longer. There are plenty of dig enlargement products that all involve stretching the penis from the outside, but nothing that addresses substantial internal growth. That's when I came up with some steps for men to follow to take their penis size back.

The Law of Use

Let's not forget the penis has muscular structure to it. It's more than that, but it's definitely got that structure, which means the more you use it the stronger it gets. Just like working your biceps in the gym, you can work your penis out too, but guess how you work it out – fucking. There's no way around it. Use it or lose it.

That said, it's not just about having sex, but how you're having sex. First of all, I suggest raw sex; meaning, no condom or material between your penis and her vagina. One of the things that helps a penis expand outward is direct contact to a vaginal wall. This of course isn't possible when the penis can't feel the wetness of the vagina.

NOTE: Each man must have sex in a way that supports his beliefs around safety from STDs and pregnancy. This advice is in no way saying you should be risky in your behavior. There are plenty of ways you can engage in raw, skin-to-skin sex without violating your own set of standards and morality. The advice here is simply matter-of-fact.

Not only should you have raw sex, but to increase girth, it's important that you have sex with women whose vagina is significantly wider than the girth of your penis. Again, this provides and opportunity for your penis to expand outward and grow to fill the size differential between you and her. Having sex with a woman with at tight vagina relative to your penis girth won't serve you in growing your penis size.

Once you're inside of her vagina you should begin to grind and stir inside of her. The goal is to keep your penis in the center of her vaginal shaft, such that your penis is equally distant from all the walls of her vagina. This will stimulate the growth outward of the penis to meet the vaginal walls. You should do this exercise for two minutes at a time and then go back to your normal stroking and lovemaking technique.

Performing this technique and set of exercise may feel weird to you and your partner. Feel free to inform your partner ahead of time that you'll be doing some exercises during your lovemaking and you'd love her support. Let her know it won't be too excessive and is supporting your penis health. In addition, these exercises will also benefit her. As your penis is growing in girth, her vagina will be tightening simultaneously, which will ultimately increase the quality of your lovemaking and sensitivity.

In terms of growing the length of your penis, I suggest you have sex with women whose vaginal canal is deeper than your penis is long. I also suggest the sex be raw for the maximum effect. Once you enter her vagina with your penis you should begin a grinding motion where you're not pumping your penis in and out of her, but simply grinding your hips and pelvis in such a way where you're attempting to go deeper inside of her. While you're doing this, you want to visualize your penis growing to meet and touch her cervix. In your mind, see the head of your penis touching (kissing) her cervix. Do this for a minute or two then go back to normal intercourse.

Just like the girth increasing exercises, the length increasing exercises will also benefit your partner by increasing the sensitivity of the deep ring around her cervix, which is the location of what some label the "deep spot." The deep spot is an extremely orgasmic set of points within a woman's vagina around the circular ring of her around her cervix. When certain points are pressed along that cervical ring, it can bring her to a very intense orgasmic state. This can be done through a finger techniques or with a penis long enough to reach her cervical ring. Either way, as you push your penis and grind in to reach her cervical ring, it will automatically begin to increase her sensitivity there.

The combination of these two exercises – girth and length – will greatly increase her sensitivity while also supporting you in your penis growth.

Again, find the partner and circumstances that feel the best for you. Find partners you can trust and communicate with and who are open to you doing this type of work. Explain the benefits for the both of you and have fun with the exercises.

Erectile Dysfunction

Let's dig in a bit deeper and discuss a major topic that millions of men are facing every year – erectile dysfunction. First let's define what it is so we're clear. I define erectile dysfunction as the state where your penis is not able to achieve a rock-hard erection during most of your sexual and intimate encounters with a variety of women.

Breaking down the definition, we have "rock-hard," which means your penis is ninety degrees or less when erect compared to your abdomen. Meaning, if you're standing up and your penis is erect and I measure the angle between your penis and your abdomen, it's ninety degrees or less. The ideal angle and the one that signifies the most health and sexual vitality is a forty-five degree angle. Not only should the angle be ninety degrees or more, but the firmness should be the consistency of wood (see the section on Firmness in this chapter). Unprocessed wood has the unique property of being hard with an exterior and interior softness to it. Unlike metal or iron, wood has a heavy water content to it, which makes it both stiff and pliable; thus, easy to shape and work with for construction. As I mentioned earlier, the trigram Sun in Feng Shui and the I Ching Oracle system is governed by the element of wood. This trigram is also a symbol of the Leader archetype, which is the King of the kingdom. The King is required to be firm, yet understanding so that all the people can feel honored equally. Without the pliability a leader turns into a dictator, which is ineffective in gaining trust and acceptance from the people. This is also why Warriors are not leaders because their lack of flexibility makes them tyrannical and hated by those they are trying to protect. The Warrior is governed by the trigram Li in Feng Shui and the I Ching Oracle system. Its element is fire, but also iron and steel.

This may seem to be a high expectation to meet regarding penis erectile health, but this is the standard for a healthy male post puberty. In addition, age doesn't play a factor here. As men, we don't adjust our measurements based on our age, but rather adjust our habits and work ethic to maintain our masculinity.

When I say "most" of your encounters, I'm saying over ninety percent of your sexual encounters should result in your penis being rock hard before, during, and for a time after sexual intercourse with a woman. Again, this is the standard we should expect of ourselves as men. The remaining ten percent is reserved for times when:

- We attempt to have sex again too soon after ejaculation.
- We are legitimately tired or exhausted due to excess energy expenditure before engaging in sex.
- Exposure to environmental conditions (i.e. extreme high or low temperatures) that remove our focus from sexual intercourse.
- Using a condom for additional rounds of sex after the initial sexual intercourse engagement.
- Sickness or illness (although, sexual arousal generally trumps most sicknesses).

The last part is also critical when I say erectile dysfunction only applies when men are unable to achieve erections with a "variety of women." In other words, you can't measure a man's erectile health against his sexual performance with only one woman. It's impossible. That's like measuring a screwdriver's performance and effectiveness using only one type of screw. Even if the performance with that one woman changes over time where once it was good or even exceptional, but has later deteriorated, you still can't judge effectively. Just like using any scientific method, we need a variety of examples and data from which to truly measure the efficacy of something.

This is the biggest issue with the men being diagnosed with

erectile dysfunction today, which is their performance sample size is too small. They are only evaluating their ability to get erect with their wives, which doesn't tell us much at all. I need for men to really understand what I'm saying here because many of us have been brainwashed into believing that if we can't achieve a healthy erection with our wives that something must be wrong with us. Nothing can be further from the truth. The truth is the penis is not a mechanical device. Erections aren't solely based on what you want to achieve in the moment. We know this for a fact because we started achieving involuntary erections from the time we were children and before we even understood what sex or attraction was in the first place.

At the most fundamental level, the male erection is based on energy. This means the combination of your level of desire and passion (vitality, energy) in conjunction with the complimentary energy of another person will have a profound effect on your physiology and energy will rush to the areas of the body where it senses the least resistance. This just so happens to be the penis for men – a fleshy organ with the capacity to grow. It's your electricity (yang chi) flowing through you as a man that is the spark and foundation of your erections, which is why we've all experienced having involuntary erections as children. But combine that with the magnetic, complimentary energy of a woman and the effects are even more intense.

Another consideration for men who've diagnosed themselves with erectile dysfunction is whether or not they experience any involuntary erections in the morning or at night while they sleep. If this is the case, you don't have erectile dysfunction. You may still have some work to do regarding your personal vitality as a man, but you don't have erectile dysfunction. Involuntary erections are a clear sign that your penis works just fine and that the problem is most likely mental. When I say mental, I'm saying your approach to having sex and your choice of partners is mostly likely at the root of your challenges.

The last part of the definition is "sexual or intimate" encounters with women because your penis should not only get hard just before sexual intercourse, but also during intimate encounters like simple touch, kissing, etc. Soft intimacy is a powerful and magnetic energy that proves to be arousing to men who are healthy.

The Elephant in the Room

Allow me to address the elephant in the room, which is most men who have erectile dysfunction either are or were married. This is problematic based on my above commentary because I'm saying you can't judge your erectile health based on just one partner sample. So the question is, how does a monogamous man who's married indulge in a larger sample size while still remaining in integrity within his marriage? The short answer is you can't unless your wife is open to the idea of you getting support through a sex worker. I don't have any answers for you and I'm not interested in beating around the bush with what men need to solve their problems. I'll leave it in your hands, as a man, to do what you must in order to properly assess yourself and deal with your erectile health. Sometimes the limits of our marriage prevent us from getting what we really need as men, but again, that's also a choice that we should be prepared to live with.

The Cure for Erectile Dysfunction

The cure for erectile dysfunction is actually very straightforward. You need to start using your penis. I mentioned before that our penises have an innate intelligence within them to the point where they know what their purpose is and how and where that purpose should be applied. To cure erectile dysfunction you need to do two things: (a) listen to your dick and (b) use it.

Part of the problem with being male in our modern society is we've become very used to suppressing our sexuality. Since grade school we've tried to hide and suppress our erections in class as if it meant there was something wrong with us. We've had to hide our attractions to women and pretend like we don't have any interest and felt absolutely nothing. We've had to act like rejection by women didn't hurt our feelings deeply and in some cases we even turned things around and got angry and aggressive. We've had to pretend we were strong when often times we were tired or weak. It's just a part of being a male-bodied human in our society. That said, it's a series of behaviors that needs to be unlearned. As men we need to learn to follow our attractions or at least acknowledge them. We need to learn to not try to justify our attractions or paint them as something they aren't. For example, when we claim a simple sexual attraction is a desire for a committed relationship when it's not.

Learn to follow the intelligence of your penis. If it responds to the redheaded woman wearing the tight pants then that's what it is. No justification needed. Feel free to let her know or don't if you're not comfortable. If your penis doesn't respond to your girlfriend on a particular night, don't try to force it. Instead, just accept it's not ready at that time and be at peace with not having intercourse that night. What you'll find is if you follow your true attractions then your penis will start to magically work again, and better than ever, I might add.

The other aspect is the law of use. If you want your penis to work effectively during intercourse then you need to make sure you're having intercourse frequently and with women you're attracted to. If you're able to do that and be at peace with your attractions then you'll find your penis working just fine.

I know I'm making these solutions sound easy and they aren't depending on your personal situation in life. I know if you're married, for example, you really don't have any integrity-based options, but instead will either need to have a really authentic conversation with your wife, accept your erectile dysfunction, or use conventional medical methods like pharmaceutical drugs to deal with the problem. The choice is yours.

Psychological Issues

Let's get into the metaphysics of lack. Whether it's money, good health, solid relationships, or penis size, there's a mental component to all of these things. Many men who have a small penis have a subconscious belief they aren't enough and don't deserve a solid sexual connection with a woman. They believe they aren't worthy and the body follows in kind by manifesting a small penis. Many of these beliefs actually hit at a young age when we're boys. Something triggers it and we just don't feel worthy of stepping into the highest levels of our sexual masculinity. We see the same thing happen for people who have money issues and a poverty mindset – they just don't feel worthy of wealth. They feel afraid to come into their financial power. The same goes for penis size.

The first step here is to adjust how you're thinking about yourself and what you deserve as a man. You have to come into your manhood in thought and action. Know you've been given everything you need to be the man you need to be. Know you deserve to be that king and warrior for women of your choosing. Forgive yourself for any perceived transgressions. Forgive your father for any ways that you may have perceived he came up short with you or your mother. Forgive your mother for any perceived trans-gressions you may have seen between her and your father or any other man. Don't allow her disappointment and anger towards men shape who you are as a man. This may be difficult for men to face, but it's true that our mothers have a profound impact on who we are as men and that our mothers are often times at the root of some of our manhood issues. If your mother had a chal-lenging time dealing with men in her life, especially your father, this could be interpreted by you as a general unworthiness of men. If you accepted this or a similar belief as a child, you may very well be punishing yourself by truncating your expression of masculinity. I can't stress this point enough. We have to grow past the belief that our mothers were infallible and remember that we're all human beings who experience pain, make mistakes, and sometimes blame others when we should be taking responsibility for our own life choices.

Again, this is a sensitive subject, but we usually hold some level of contempt for our parents. It's the child within us that wants to blame some of our shortcomings on them and what they didn't do for us. It's okay. This book isn't about blame, but about identifying the source of our challenges as men and addressing them expe-ditiously so we can get on with the lives we desire. Don't take any of this personally. Don't get down on yourself because you hold your mother or father to blame for your personal situation in life. Accept it and move on.

Our bodies can transform and change in any way we'd like them too, but we must have a belief in that ability. We must be willing to deal with the subconscious programs and patterns at the root of our physiology. Every part of us as men is a result of subconscious belief that has manifested itself as our body. This goes to why some men can't get or stay in shape. They may start out working out, but can't maintain their exercise regime. Why? Because they don't believe they can have or even deserve to express themselves in a physically powerful masculine way. Again, this is a belief that came from childhood. Even if you've been in shape before, but later lost it shows you don't have a belief you deserve it. The same thing happens to people around health and money. Rich one day, filing bankruptcy the next.

I can't stress enough how penis size is largely mental. That may sound strange because every other part of our bodies seem to be sourced from a physical blueprint, but this is only partly true for the penis. When you look at the human body, in most cases all of its parts are proportional to everything else. I know there are exceptions, like someone's nose or ears being proportionally larger than the rest of their face. Occasionally, you see someone with excessively long arms compared to their body, but all in all most human beings are very evenly proportioned.

This actually isn't the case when it comes to the human penis. It's very common to have a man who's over six feet five to have a small penis or a man who's five foot four with a massively large penis. If you're not familiar with this, I suggest you talk to multiple women that you trust about their experiences with men. You can also ask a sex worker who is willing to talk about her client experiences. Ask her about the variety of penis sizes with men relative to their heights and what will be revealed is a number of cases where the proportions were grossly misrepresented compared to the rest of the body. The penis is an intelligent organ with a unique and massively important function in the procreation process. From that standpoint, it can be said it's been given some special and autonomous powers to fulfill its mission.

There's no organ on the male human body that changes and transforms as much as the penis. It's size and shape differential throughout the day, even outside of sex, can vary by inches in length and several millimeters in girth. It's a highly sensitive organ that responds to our mind, our body, and our environment. We often attempt to simplify the penis as either just something that hangs there or something that's like a piece of wood when erect, but nothing can be further from the truth. It harbors its own intelligence and unique set of functional traits.

These observations alone should help you see the penis as unique and potentially highly pliable. We're not talking about a finger here or a leg, which has a bone base; thus, making the possibilities of growth more involved. Take some time to meditate on how your penis has functioned over your adult lifetime and come to the realization that it can and will respond seamlessly to your thoughts. The more we heal the mind, the more our penis will respond to our will.

Do this exercise as a beginning to address your psychological blocks around penis size.

Psychological Exercise One

Go into a state of trance. This is best done by sitting down and meditating. Once you feel your consciousness withdrawing from the physical environment around you and being more focused inward, begin to visualize yourself standing in a field with tall grass, a nice breeze, and the sun shining on your face. See yourself standing with your eyes closed, back straight, with your legs shoulder width apart, and your chin slightly tilted downward. Feel yourself taking take breaths in the vision where you're breathing in through your nose and your abdomen is expanding outward and breathing out and your abdomen is collapsing. Feel the heat from the sun shining brightly on your forehead. You body starts to heat up and as it does, feel your entire body start to grow taller. Feel and see your body getting taller and taller as you begin to grow upward toward the sun. Eventually see your head in the clouds. Now, inside of the vision, open your eyes and look down at the earth around you. Feel how amazing if feels to be a giant on the earth. Continue to feel the warmth of the sun on your entire body. Now feel the sun's energy heating up your heart and powering the blood flow through your body. Next, feel the sunlight heating up your penis and testicles causing them to grow and throb with power. Allow yourself to feel it fully and enjoy the sensation. Continue this vision for as long as comfortable. When you're ready, slowly come out of trance and back into your body. Open your eyes and journal any insights that may have come to you.

Take your time with yourself and be patient and gentle. This is delicate work. Otherwise our penises are just some extra appendage, without a profound purpose in our lives. It's the most important psychological organ to man. It occupies every aspect of our lives and therefore our psychological relationship to it should be treated with care and seriousness.

What's Your Angle?

First of all, your penis should be able to stand at a ninety-degree angle from your torso when it's erect when you're standing. Meaning the angle between your erect penis and your stomach should be ninety degrees or less when you are standing straight with both feet on the floor.

How do we know ninety-degrees or less is the proper angle? All you have to do is remember when you were sixteen when the angle was more like fifty degrees off your belly. At that age you could practically fuck yourself in the navel with no hands while standing straight up. Or if you masturbated and shot off, the semen would hit you in the chin or chest or something if you didn't point it away from your body frame. Remember masturbating vertically instead of horizontally? It would look like you're using one of those shake weights. That's the angle I'm talking about. When you get older and start to lose your energy you masturbate either out (horizontally) or down towards the floor because your angle is like 115°.

I use the age of sixteen because it represents a snapshot of yourself before your bad habits and errors of living caught up with you. We have to realize that age has nothing to do with health so much as your ability to live correctly and manage the resources you've been given. Again, as we neglect our bodies it begins to lose energy and that's why we begin to lose functionality over particular resources. You can also look at the artwork of ancient Egypt and other eastern civilizations and see the nude male depictions. These dudes were never greater than ninety degrees and these were grown men not boys. Some of the statues had their rock-hard penises almost like an attachment to their abdomen. It looked like it would have to be surgically removed to separate it from his stomach. I'm talking zero degrees here.

But also if you think about sexual positions a hard penis at less than ninety degrees is what's required to make things work. Think about the missionary position. If I'm lying down over top of a woman, a ninety-degree or more penis angel is not going to cut it, especially, if it's rock hard. A forty-five degree angle works the best actually. That's how a penis can go directly into a wet vagina without any hand assistance or guidance. Hand guidance of a penis is a human phenomenon. I've never seen any animal use his hand or paw or whatever to guide a cock into a pussy. Have you?

A rock hard cock at the right angle will enter a wet pussy without any problems every time. This is not just a human phenomenon with the forty-five degree angle as we see in the animal world. Have you ever seen lions fucking? The female lion lies down on her stomach and all four legs and sticks her ass in the air and the male lion comes behind her and shoves his cock in her pussy. The male lion is not using his paws to guide his penis. He's just shoving it in, but to do this he has to be at about thirty-five to forty-five degrees off of his torso. Even when a woman is on top of a man, forty-five degrees works best. When she is on top of the man she leans forward to the point where she can almost kiss him and his cock slides right in. For a woman to sit down on a hard penis at ninety-degrees is awkward at best. It doesn't look natural or smooth. The only position that works for the ninety-degree penis is a woman laying on a bed or table and the man walking straight at her to insert his penis, but that's a rare position.

Firmness

Next is the firmness of the penis. Again, remembering back at a younger age when erections were frequent and new, a penis was about as hard as a lead pipe. That's when your cock was so hard it would try to release itself from you body and attack the first thing it could stick its head into. An erect penis would be so hard that you had to put it somewhere to soften it up a bit because it literally hurt to a degree. Hard and heavy like you could hit someone on the back of the head with it and knock them out cold. It was a wonder actually that something so fleshy and with no bones inside of it could be as hard as metal and not only was it hard, but it felt hard and not just to the touch. An erect penis would become one of the hardest parts of our body next to teeth. Think about it, harder than a leg or an arm or finger or whatever. It was the hardest thing we had.

A firm penis feels like it's about to bust through the skin. It feels like it needs more space to expand and the skin wrapped around it is restricting it in some sick and painful way. You remember what that feels like, right? Well, if you don't have that feeling knock a few points off your firmness scale. Next, it has to feel hard to the touch. Literally, it should feel like a bedpost or any smooth piece of rounded wood. Wood is hard to the touch, but it also has an underlying softness to it in its energetic makeup. It's kind of hard to describe, but compare the firmness of a wood piece and a lead pipe of the same size and shape. The lead pipe has a density and heaviness to it as well as less give. As a matter of fact, one of the primary masculine character types is that of leadership. In the Chinese Bagua astrological system (I wrote a book on this called the *Bagua Character Map: Science, Analysis & Interpretation* that is super complicated – you've been warned) the trigram Sun (pronounced "soon") governs leadership and is represented by the mature wood element; whereas, the primary feminine element is metal and is governed by the trigram Chien. So when you think of masculinity think about the elements of mature wood, like redwood trees, fire, dry earth, and dry air.

When an erect penis is inside of a woman she should be able to feel it pulsating inside of her as if it wants to expand and push out her vaginal walls. This sensation should be both voluntary and involuntary. Voluntary meaning when a man does his kegel perineum muscle squeezes his penis expands outward. The penis should also be able to withstand a woman's kegel squeezes. Again she should feel like she is squeezing a wood stick inside of her vagina.

Kegels

For those unfamiliar with the kegel exercises these are fairly basic. There is a muscle halfway between your anus and scrotum called the perineum. In Chinese medicine the spot is denoted by the Hui Yin acupuncture point. You can easily find this muscle by attempting the cut the flow of urine off midstream. The muscle you squeeze to accomplish this task is the same muscle used to perform the male kegel exercises. The kegel exercises will strengthen the entire muscle network supporting your reproductive system. These muscles influence penis angle off the torso as well as penis firmness. Other benefits of these exercises are prolonged sexual intercourse without ejaculation and increased mental control during sex and in general. The kegel exercises should also assist with the natural energy flow into the penis, which is another indication of your sexual health as a man. Here are some basic kegel exercises…

Kegel Exercise One

If this is your first time performing kegel exercises or if this is your first time performing these exercises in over two months then start with Kegel Exercise One and stop for the day. Do not go to another kegel exercise in the same day.

Step One: Squeeze the perineum for one second and immediately release.

Step Two: Repeat this squeeze and release twenty times and then rest.

Note: If this is your first month performing these exercises do not go beyond twenty reps. Do not do more kegel exercises for the rest of the day. Rest is critical for these exercises. DO NOT GO BEYOND THE RECOMMENDED REPS.

Kegel Exercise Two

If this is your first time performing kegel exercises or if this is your first time performing these exercises in over two months then start with Kegel Exercise One and stop for the day. Do not go to another kegel exercise in the same day. Once you have finished Kegel Exercise One then you can move to Kegel Exercise Two the next day if desired.

- Step One: Squeeze the perineum for five seconds and then release.
- Step Two: Squeeze the perineum for one second and release.
- Step Three: Repeat Step Two four additional times.
- Step Four: Repeat Steps One and Two four additional times.
- Step Five: Rest.

Note: If this is your first month performing these exercises do not go beyond twenty reps. Do not do more kegel exercises for the rest of the day. Rest is critical for these exercises. DO NOT GO BEYOND THE RECOMMENDED REPS.

Kegel Exercise Three

If this is your first time performing kegel exercises or if this is your first time performing these exercises in over two months then start with Kegel Exercise One and stop for the day. Do not go to another kegel exercise in the same day. Once you have finished Kegel Exercise One then you can move to Kegel Exercise Two the next day if desired and then to Kegel Exercise Three.

- Step One: Squeeze the perineum for ten seconds and then release.
- Step Two: Squeeze the perineum for one second and release.
- Step Three: Repeat Step Two nine additional times.
- Step Four: Repeat Steps One and Two four additional times.
- Step Five: Rest.

Note: If this is your first month performing these exercises do not go beyond the fifty reps assigned in the directions. Do not do more kegel exercises for the rest of the day. Rest is critical for these exercises. DO NOT GO BEYOND THE RECOMMENDED REPS.

Kegel Exercise Four

Once you have worked these exercises for a month or more, you may begin to do multiple exercises throughout the day. You may also improvise your own exercises as you see fit. You should still be aware of staying within your limits. Do not overwork these exercises.

Understanding the Erection

An erection for a man has nothing to do with a woman or sex or any of that. An erect penis is an indication of a man's overall power and vitality, his available energy and zealousness. What wakes a healthy man up in the morning? An erect penis. Not the need to urinate or the alarm clock. Have you ever tried to sleep with a hard-on? It's like trying to drive your car with a boot on it. You just can't do it. The erection is pulling you out the bed. It's talking to you like, "*Let's go get em chief!*" The only thing that stops you from getting out the bed with a hard dick is if a woman is lying next to you. Instead of getting out of the bed you are basically rolling over. But, that's actually a waste of energy because that hard on represents your ability to conquer. The girl lying next to you is not what you're looking to conquer. Not that she, or you for that matter, won't appreciate some roll over fun, but we are talking about something bigger here.

The hard on has nothing to do with her even if she thinks it does or if you do. That's your body's way of saying, "*Yo, we are fully recharged and ready to take on anything coming our way. Especially, those things we were dreaming about last night. Let's do this.*" If your cock is not hard in the morning upon waking there is a definite problem and don't give me the old age bit. This is a definite sign of stress and lack of regenerative ability within the body. And fucking the night before has nothing to do with it. You should be able to have sex at night and still wake up with a hard-on. If not, it means you went past your limits for the day. You used more energy resources than you could replace based on your nutrient intake and sleep efficiency.

It's just important for men to understand this. An erection is in no way related to women or sex in and of itself. It's totally related to your desire to achieve what you want as well as your general reproductive health. Your dick gets hard because you want the woman. That's how it works. Whatever you want badly enough will give you a hard-on. It doesn't seem like it because we've become conditioned to erections related to sex only, but it's not natural. That's why men have issues getting hard later in life because it's hard (no pun) to support an artificial stimulus over an extended period of time. I know that may be difficult to understand or believe, but go back to your early teenage years and count the number of erections you got throughout the day that were totally unrelated to the girls in the classroom. For me it was all of them. I would be falling asleep in class only to be awakened by my penis banging against the bottom of the desk or trying to rip my pants open at the crotch. I remember thinking, what is wrong with me? I'm hard for no reason. This sucks.

Teacher: "*Carl, please come to the board and demonstrate solving for X in this algebraic equation.*"

Me: "*Um. I'll take an 'F' please. Just fail me for the semester.*"

Teacher: "*Ok wise guy, go to the principle's office and let's see if he can straighten out that little attitude of yours.*"

Me: "*Actually, I'm straight enough already. Can I just sit here and write one million times I will listen to the teacher or maybe I can sit here and think for a while and contemplate my folly. You see this is a serious issue for me. When I was a boy my mother told me to be my own person, take risks, but honor your elders. The more I thought about those words, the more I wondered how I could live up to them.*" Ok, I need to buy about three more minutes before I stand up. What else can I talk about? Think Carl, think. Oh, yeah. "*Our founding fathers had a vision for our country that included free thought and the expansion of freedoms for all peoples. As I read the Declaration of Independence it inspired me to be a better citizen and that's what I plan to do...*"

Teacher: Calling the Principle's office. "*Yes, this is Mrs. Templeton in room 101. We have a child here under the influence of some heavy psychedelic and hallucinogenic drugs. Can you send security right away? Thanks.*"

It didn't matter that I got the suspension. I'll take anything other than standing up with a hard-on bulging through my pants. Seriously, I'll take lashes in the school parking lot after the dismissal bell. The whole school can watch as long as my cock is soft and neatly tucked in my jeans.

So to make a long story short, you should get a number of erections throughout the day if your reproductive system is healthy. That's just the way it is. Do I have a number of times? No. But, I would go back to your childhood (mentally of course) and get a visual of how often you got hard-ons throughout the day and use that as a measure for starters.

It's in the Sperm

We can also look at the quality and quantity of your sperm upon ejaculation. The quality of seminal fluid should be of medium density. What the means is the seminal fluid itself should be the same consistency of the slime in okra, but not quite as sticky. The consistency is medium, meaning, not too runny like water and not too thick like glue, but in between. The runny seminal fluid indicates a lower sperm count and less nutritive fluids, which provide protection and nutrition for the sperm to live on until they get into the egg. The thicker seminal fluid represents and excess of waste products and hampers the sperms ability to grow and thrive once ejaculated from the penis.

In addition, upon ejaculation, it should shoot at least a few feet out of shaft of the penis and it doesn't matter if it shoots vertically or horizontally, there should be some force behind your ejaculations. Now, this force is not directly related to the health of the sperm, but ties back into the state of your energy. It's the expulsion of energy out of the body that propels the seminal fluid through the shaft of the penis. Yes, the heavier and thicker the seminal fluid the more power needed to expel it, so from that standpoint seminal density does play a role. But let's not confuse these two components: (a) your internal power and (b) seminal density.

At this point, lets take a minute to understand the makeup of seminal fluid. I won't go into the details because you can look that information up online. But seminal fluid is made up of sperm and nutritive fluid that supports the sperm in summary. So you have life in the sperm and what that life needs in order to subsist. When we discuss seminal fluid we are primarily talking about the nutritive supporting fluid as opposed to the sperm itself. This nutritive fluid is difficult to make and is one of the most rich and nutritive substances your body makes which is why the quality of it can vary so dramatically depending upon the health of the person producing it. Sperm need this substance to live. It's like comparing fish to water or humans to air. The living organism can't exist without its environment. If your body cannot produce this nutritive substance it won't produce sperm. If your body doesn't produce sperm there's no need for an erect penis and the body won't channel any energy there. It has to be noted that this seminal fluid is not just produced for procreation. Again, it goes back to your ability as a man to achieve in the world. This fluid is necessary to power you towards your goals and objectives. The intense energy given off by this nutritive substance is used by the body to fuel the attainment of your aspirations. It's an energy source for you too.

We often times hear doctors talk about sperm count and how that's important for you to get a woman pregnant. Sperm count is also used to measure the success of a vasectomy in males. Sperm count basically measures the volume of sperm in a man's ejaculate – the more sperm, the more potent the male. But sperm count goes back to the nutritive seminal fluid we just discussed. The body will only produce enough sperm as can be supported by the amount of food it can make to support it. So if you are generally unhealthy you won't be able to produce this fluid and will have a low sperm count. So, yes, sperm count is an excellent indicator of sexual and general health; however, it's important that we understand the link to this nutritive substance.

The other indicators of seminal fluid quality besides thickness would be the smell, color, and texture. Seminal fluid should have a slightly sweet smell to it, as fructose is a main component of the nutritive substance supporting the sperm. If the smell is rancid or sour it's an indication of excessive waste material in the seminal fluid along with an imbalanced bacteria count and pH levels. The same holds true for the color of the seminal fluid. A healthy color is a bright white or a slightly off-white or light yellow color. Anything else indicates an imbalance.

Perineum Muscle and Constitution

I mentioned earlier that an erect penis should grow inside of a wet vagina. It may be difficult to notice this during sexual intercourse because so much is going on, but you may notice over time, changes in the size of your penis. This growth is correlated to the strength of the perineum muscles, but is also tied to the indwelling intelligence inherent to the human body and specifically the penis in this case. I've talked to a number of women that have said their boyfriend's penis has increased in size after a while of having steady intercourse. This is an example of the penis expanding outward even though in this example it happens over time. The bottom line is the penis does grow to not only accommodate the vagina, but to interact with it. If the man's penis is already filling up the woman's vagina then growth is unlikely, as the woman's vagina will most likely expand to make the adjustment, but for men with smaller penises compared to their girlfriends vaginas, growth is inevitable when having raw sex; meaning, the skin of the penis interacts directly with the walls of the vagina.

Another way to measure the perineum muscle strength is your ability to hold off ejaculation. How do you do it? The same way you hold urine, by squeezing this muscle at key times during intercourse. Let me say this right now so no one gets confused. I said squeezing the perineum during keys times during intercourse. For those who haven't strengthened this muscle and think they can wait until they have a strong urge to ejaculate – ah, negative. Once your perineum is strong enough then yes, but until then, waiting until the end is pointless. You might as well just let loose the juice. You can test this strength by holding in your urine. If you can cut it off instantly with no trailing stream and no dripping then your muscle is strong. If it takes a few seconds to completely stop the urine then you have work to do. That was easy, right? I just don't believe there are any mysteries in life. True, we may not know things, but it doesn't mean the answer is not readily available. Usually, our issue is knowing what questions to ask as opposed to finding the answers we need.

Another measure of perineum strength is your ability to stay erect inside of a vagina for an extended period of time. Fucking is not a sprint (unless you're working on a quickie); it's a marathon, or at least a 5k run. Anyone who's had sex for over an hour knows that a number of different factors come into play including your ability to stay erect and her ability to stay wet. It's common for men to begin to get soft during sexual intercourse and for women to dry out. Why does this happen? For one thing, the desire begins to die down. The truth is having sex can get boring after a while. I know I've faked ejaculations to end sex and women do the same thing all the time. They'll fake an orgasm to get this dude up off of them. Sex gets boring when it's purely physical as opposed to energetic. When sex is purely physical it gets boring, like running laps around a track or riding a bike. After a while you just want to get off and do something else. When sex is energetic it consistently escalates to higher and higher levels. I discuss this in more detail in the male orgasm section.

As mentioned before when describing the reason for why a penis gets erect, when we don't desire something we have no zealousness, enthusiasm and thus energy to make it happen. Without energy pointing the way a penis can't get or stay erect. This explains why men may lose an erection during sex. This also explains why men and women expand the physical bounds during sex as a means to keep it exciting. Anything from hair pulling, to choking, to slapping, to anal sex, titty fucking, to oral or whatever. Hey, I'm not busting on anyone's sexual preference or technique, but the fact is that more physical variety is needed when the energy and excitement itself is absent. When you talk to the Tantra masters they will tell you that sexual intercourse has very little movement. It involves the man's penis inside the woman's vagina and them sitting still in a state of deep meditation and bliss for hours. Is there any movement? Yes, of course, but movement is not the focus and not the source of the pleasure. It's simply used to adjust one's position and to create enough friction to maintain moisture and hardness for the woman and man when necessary. The old school Tantra masters are hardcore. Most folks just wouldn't last under their tutelage, at least not in this day and age.

But in the case of extreme friction sexual intercourse for an extended period of time a man should be able to maintain his erection. An inability to do that may indicate not only perineum muscle weakness, but also a general lack of vitality and cardiovascular strength. In addition, the loss of an erection may be an indication of a weak immune system. Over time, the man may get too hot or too cold and the body is forced to shift energetic resources away from the penis and reproductive system in order to protect itself from illness or viral imbalances.

After you have had sexual intercourse and ejaculated how long should it take you to recover and have sex again? The answer is it depends. I know that doesn't help, but it does depend. The more you ejaculate the longer the recovery time, but a healthy male having sex three to five times per week, where he ejaculates all but one of those times, should be able to recover from sex within five to fifteen minutes. Now, let me add some caveats. A prerequisite is that the man wants to have sex again in terms of genuine desire. Remember, a genuine desire and passion are required to channel energy into the penis. Wanting to have sex because your girlfriend wants to, when in fact you don't, is not a desire to have sex and will rarely yield a quick recovery time. When you desire to have sex the recovery time is less. I can't stress how important this point is. Because often times men think there is something wrong with them because they can't get hard again when their girlfriends want to have sex. Nope, there's nothing wrong with you my friend. You just don't want to have sex and can't bring yourself to tell her. It's not because you don't love her or aren't attracted to her, it's because you don't have the passion for her in the moment. It's hard to desire something with a strong zealousness when it's plentiful. It's like having a passion for oxygen. You can't have a passion for it because it's bountiful. How about one million in cash, or the new Benz, or the woman in apartment 4b? Now you're talking. So if you want the pussy, like really want it, then you should be able to get hard again in short order unless you've been having marathon sex over the past few days.

Long Distance

As stated earlier, it's the prana shakti that is the energy responsible for propelling the semen out of the penis. This is the essence of the male inner force and is an indicator of his inner fortitude. It reflects his ability to have an impact in the world and affect change. A measurement of this inner fortitude is measured by his ability to shoot his semen over a long distance. A factor in shooting distance will be the density and quantity of the semen as mentioned before. That said, you should be able to fire some cum shots a minimum of two feet, three to four if you're Hercules in this mother. As I said earlier, it will vary for a number of reasons, but let's keep it real for a moment. Semen dribbling out of your penis like someone coughing up blood is not a good look. You're designed to shoot semen not dribble and drool it out the cock. That's just the way it is. There's no need to get tape measures out and practice. You should be able to feel it for the most part. We all know a dribble versus a shot. Not only that, but an ejaculation from masturbation is not as powerful as an ejaculation from sexual intercourse. I'm not sure if folks have realized this, but masturbation and intercourse are not equivalent in the least. Your body is not going to respond in the same way to those two stimuli. Plus, the passion factor kicks in as well. We just aren't as excited to masturbate as we are to dive head first into some new pussy. That's just the way it is. What man turns a woman down to go masturbate instead?

Woman: "*How about you come back to my place so I can suck and fuck you until you go blind?*"

Man: "*Nah. I was planning to masturbate to my favorite porno flick. Plus, I just bought this new super lubricant and can't wait to try it out. Hopefully, it will prevent these calluses I've been getting. Thanks, though."*

General Fitness

Lastly, we can't ignore being physically fit as an indication of sexual health. Yes, fitness is a general indicator of health, but fucking when you're out of shape sucks. If you don't believe me, try it for yourself. When you're out of shape, you cum quicker, are softer, and shoot shorter than when you're in shape. That's just the facts about it. Cardiovascular fitness also affects your recovery time and your ability to produce semen. The healthier you are the more your body wants to procreate. When you're healthy your body wants to procreate bad and feels it has the right and duty to do it in a big way. This is definitely one you can try for yourself and see that everything across the board is impacted by your physical fitness. Earlier I spoke about leadership as an essential component to manhood. One of the primary qualities of being a leader is your cardiovascular strength, which translates into your ability to synthesize oxygen. The best true leaders are those with the greatest ability to synthesize oxygen, whether they were born with this ability due to a healthy cardiovascular system, or if they worked themselves into that state of health.

Flexibility

Last but certainly not least is flexibility during sex. No, not willingness to try new positions, but your ability to be in them. There's a difference between desire and ability. Stiffness is a sign of energy loss and aging. A big complaint from women who are sexually active and open is that some men lack physical flexibility. They complain these men can't bend their legs, backs, open their legs, etc. and I know what their saying. I've seen men have sex like that on porno movies and they just can't get anything done. A lack of flexibility greatly affects your ability to be present with women during sex. If you know you're not flexible you will be less likely to move into positions your partner desires you to move into because it will be uncomfortable or even painful for you. I'm not saying you need to be a gymnast or yogi, but touching your toes or reaching for the sky or crouching into a cannon ball position shouldn't be too much to ask.

There's a perception out there amongst men that women prefer men who are buffed with thick muscular builds. But that's actually a misperception that both men and women have. In actuality women prefer thinner strong and wiry men who have muscle density as opposed to muscle girth. If you're too muscular it's hard to fuck. You can barely turn yourself around let alone your partner. If you're thin and wiry you can fit and flip anywhere. When you have that added strength along with that wiry build it allows you to get into places and positions you would never expect to be in and simultaneously apply your strength and power. That feels good to women.

If you happen to be a big muscular man it doesn't mean women don't find you attractive, but it does mean you need to be mindful of your flexibility and movement quickness in tight spaces. The added girth of a muscular man can hamper his effectiveness during sexual intercourse without special consideration. This flexibility issue extends beyond sex. It's just important to your life in general, so be mindful of it.

An example of flexibility would be your ability to change positions without withdrawing your penis from a woman's vagina. I should be able to go from missionary to doggy-style, to her on top, to lotus, to side shots, and whatever, without pulling out of the pussy. I'm not saying not to pull out, but it should be a choice and not a necessity.

Also, you should be able to do more than perpendicular pumps in the pussy during sex. Men need to be able to move in a variety of directions and angles to be most effective. The energetic pleasure of sex has nothing to do with the pumping action; therefore, it loses its effectiveness and pleasurable feeling in short order. Don't get me wrong, it has its place, but it's only one dimension of fucking. Once inside the pussy you should be able to fuck up, down, side to side, down and up, half stroke, or whatever. Just in and out blasting is not going to cut it, trust me.

MEASURING MALE SEXUAL VITALITY

CHAPTER 19

THE ART OF MASTURBATION

LISTEN, I'M NOT HERE to tell you how to masturbate. That doesn't even feel right to me. I teach a number of classes around intimacy and sexuality, but I will never have a class on the art of masturbation. There are plenty of people and videos out there you can tap into if you really don't have a clue. If I did have a class, I wonder how it would go?

Me (Instructor): "*Ok men. With your right hand grab your penis. Make sure you leave your nut sack hanging completely exposed and untouched. If you're experiencing pain or excess friction during any part of this exercise, add more baby oil, but not too much because some friction is needed for you to feel sensation. Also make sure your towels are over your left shoulder so you can grab it when you need it.*"

Student 1: "*Should we grab the head or the shaft of the penis?*"

Me (Instructor): "*The base of the shaft.*"

"*You have to make sure there's enough spacing between each of you. I don't want anyone in someone else's line of fire. We're not responsible for dry cleaning any clothes here at the center so make sure you have a good five foot radius around all sides of you.*"

"*Now turn to page sixty-four in the magazine you were given at the beginning of class. You should see a thick caramel-colored honey with a set of double Ds, and two beach balls hiding inside of each of her butt cheeks. Gentlemen, she wants you and I mean bad.*"

Student 2: "*Am I looking at her breasts or ass to get aroused?*"

Me (Instructor): "*Son if you have to ask me that question then we have a larger issue on our hands. But to answer your question, whatever is most appealing; both if you need to."*

"Begin stroking in steady rhythmic motions until the blood begins to rush into your penis. Great technique, Sam. You've improved from last week; I can tell you're working on this at home."

"George loosen your grip a bit. It looks like you're trying to choke the life out of your penis. This isn't Murder She Wrote. *The head of your penis is turning purple cause you're cutting the blood supply off. Okay, that's better."*

"Tony, not so fast. You don't get speed points in this class plus at that rate you'll pull a muscle in your arm or your shoulder may lock up. This is a marathon not a sprint, plus we haven't spread the towels on the floor yet and I know you don't want mop duty again this week."

"Jeff, don't just work the shaft. Give the head some attention too. That's better."

"Okay fellas, I want to hear those moans and groans. Who's feeling good?"

Students Together: *"We are!"*

Me (Instructor): *"Remember when we're done here no shaking hands or slapping five with your classmates. If you need to connect with your classmates before you can get to a sink with warm water and soap, do fist bumps only. That's very important. We have extra wet wipes and hand sanitizer up front for those who need it."*

Nah, I'll leave that to certified masturbation professionals. I'm just not qualified for all of that. Plus, I just can't get motivated for a job that involves watching twenty guys with their cocks in their hand. If I wanted to see that I would go to the men's room at professional basketball game.

I haven't masturbated much in my lifetime. I promise. We can even shake on it. No? Well, you'll just have to take my word for it then. Part of that was because it was a taboo thing amongst my friends when I was growing up. They had all these demeaning names for masturbating and whenever someone was caught or suspected of masturbating they usually had hell to pay amongst their peers. Some of the terms were spanking the monkey, choking the chicken, beating your meat, beating off, massaging your muscle, milking the weasel, slapping the salami, smacking off, stroking the sausage, tugging the turkey, whacking the wiener, waxing the carrot, the five-knuckle-shuffle, jacking off, and the list goes on. The point is these weren't terms to help you feel good about touching yourself. They were terms to make you feel ashamed about it. As a result of trying to be cool, I remember specifically trying to keep the masturbating to a minimum. The mere thought of everyone at school; especially, the girls, knowing I was at home masturbating every night was too much to even think about. I'll just figure something else out.

The other reason I didn't masturbate much throughout my life is because starting at age eighteen I started getting steady streams of pussy coming my way. There's no need to masturbate when there's a girl in your bed every night. Actually, after high school I never ever thought about masturbation. Why ever do it? If you're horny, get some pussy or at least some head. See that? Problem solved.

It wasn't until I entered a long-term relationship with Southern Bella that any type of touching myself with any kind of consistency came (no pun) into the picture. Whenever we made love over the phone or via video chat, self-touching suddenly came into play and it was really nice. Really, really nice.

But just because I didn't do it much growing up doesn't mean it's not important when done in the right way and the proper frequency. The right way means that each time you do it you learn something about yourself and grow in your sexual maturity. Can you do it just for fun and because it feels good? Yes, you can. But remember that sex with the self is the same as sex with a partner in that it can have the same types of benefits and dangers. Some of the dangers include over-masturbation, which means you will tend to use it as a coping mechanism. Masturbation should not be used as a substitute for sex with a partner in my opinion. Rather it's more of a tool for self-exploration, understanding one's pleasure threshold, and pampering. Masturbating too often can lead to desensitization to vaginal intercourse with your partner as the penis can become conditioned to respond pleasurably to the touch of the hand.

In summary, here's what I think is important when it comes to masturbation for men:

- It's okay to do it and nothing to feel ashamed about.
- It shouldn't only be done with pornography as this can take away from some of the benefit of learning about yourself as well as the intimacy of it.
- Don't overdo it; otherwise, you may become conditioned to respond only to masturbation as opposed to intercourse or oral sex.
- Take time to really feel the intricacies of your body. This is not a race.
- Make it about more than just the penis. You can touch other parts of your body as well during masturbation. Make it a whole body experience.
- Don't make it ejaculation centered. Enjoy the feeling through-

out the experience instead of just looking forward to ejaculating. This will help you with orgasm.

- You don't always have to ejaculate; especially when there isn't a strong urge to do so. However, if you go too far you may experience pain in the form of "blue balls," if you don't ejaculate. I advise ejaculating if you have a long session with yourself just to be sure you're not in pain later.

CONCLUSION

WE'RE ALL ON OUR own very special and personal journeys in life and only we can define what that journey consists of. Only we can walk the many paths that awaken us to our highest potential. The goal of this book was simply to give you some insight into a possible direction for your life's journey, especially, around your sexuality as a man.

If we can learn to be present with our lovers and during our sexual encounters we'll find the clues that lead us to a greater connection and fulfilling experience. But doing that takes awareness. We have to acknowledge our sexuality as something powerful and important in our lives and worth improving. We have to understand that enhancing our sexual abilities improves the level of sexual healing we provide to others and increases our happiness and fulfillment overall. This fact alone can improve the quality of our lives.

There's a basic rule in life that says – there are no limits to what we can experience and achieve. There is no absolute best or final completion when it comes, especially to our sexuality. Ancient cultures, like the Dravidians, dedicated their entire spiritual lives attempting to unlock the secrets of human sexuality and how it could benefit their life journeys.

If we can manage to keep an open mind and ignore the limitations that pornography and mass media bombard us with on a daily basis, we should at least have an opportunity to reach new heights. Be patient with yourself in all you do and have compassion for those around you.

All things contribute to our growth and wellbeing.

ABOUT THE AUTHOR

CARL E. STEVENS, JR. (aka Rakhem Seku) is a metaphysician, life and love coach, and author. He teaches the Bagua Astrology System (BAS) and applies metaphysical concepts to support people in creating the lives they desire through the JujuMama Love Academy (JLA) – a metaphysical school he created with his wife Kenya Stevens.

Carl is the author of numerous books, including:

- *The Art of Open Relating: Volume 1 – Theory, Philosophy, & Foundation*
- *Tame Your Woman: Become the Man She Needs*
- *Manifesting Marriage for Women: 9 Steps to Finding Your Partner and Creating a Successful Marriage*
- *I Create My Life: Manifesting Your Desires Using the Sun Cycle*
- *Bagua Astrology Oracle Interpretation Guide*
- *Bagua Astrology Character Mapping Interpretation Guide*
- *Bagua Character Map: Science, Analysis, & Interpretation*
- *Moon Manifestation System Workbook & Journal*
- *Bagua Astrology for Beginners*

At the JujuMama Love Academy (JLA), students are certified in the many disciplines Carl and Kenya have created and authored including:

- Life & Love Coaching Certification
- Feminine Power Certification
- i2Tantra Certification
- Moon Manifestation System Certification
- Bagua Astrology System (BAS) Certification
- Three Way Mirror Certification

Carl and Kenya have hundreds of audios and videos available

to their students at the JLA RESOURCE LIBRARY and additional products available to the general public through their store.

Carl has been on numerous television and radio shows including:

- The Monique ShowTM
- The Ricki Lake ShowTM
- The Dr. Phil ShowTM
- The Brian Cunningham ShowTM
- Fox NewsTM, ABC NewsTM
- The Michael BaisdenTM radio show,
- Power 99FMTM in Philadelphia and many others.

Carl and Kenya have been married for over twenty years and continue to raise three children together. Carl has two degrees: a Bachelors of Science degree in Industrial Engineering from North Carolina State University and an MBA with a finance concentration from Howard University. He's worked for one of the largest consulting firms in the world for ten years doing software implementation and project management for their Fortune 100 clients.

To contact Carl, you can email him at mail@jujumama.com.

You can find his Facebook fan page at http://www.facebook.com/rakhemseku.

The website for JujuMama is http://www.jujumama.com

The website for the JujuMama Love Academy is located at http://jujumamaloveacademy.com.

The JujuMama Love Academy

Become a member of the JujuMama Love Academy (JLA) where you'll have access to people who are working to improve their relationships, sexuality, and power to manifest their lives. The membership levels are BRONZE, SILVER, and GOLD. Go to http://jujumamaloveacademy.com to sign up and see a full list of classes and certifications.

i2Tantra Certification Course

Men and women should consider taking our premier sexuality and Tantra class called i2Tantra. It will teach you to master your sexuality and support your partners and lovers in achieving their highest levels of orgasmic pleasure.

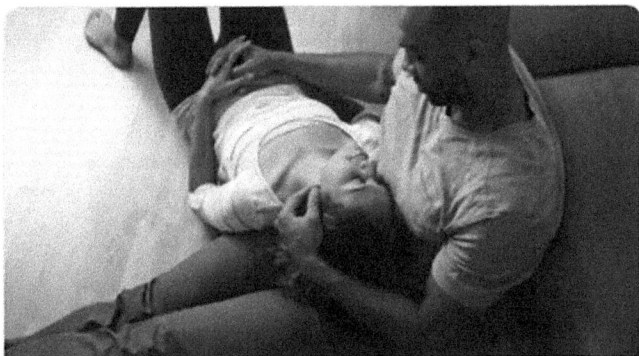

i2 Tantra Certification Course

Carl Stevens and Kenya K. Stevens   **$999**

The Art of Open Relating: Volume 1 – Theory, Philosophy, & Foundation

Continue your learning experience by reading The Art of Open Relating: Volume 1: Theory, Philosophy, & Foundation in order to continue to relationship studies. Examine the additional relationship styles available and determine if a freedom-based relating model is right for you.

Available on Amazon

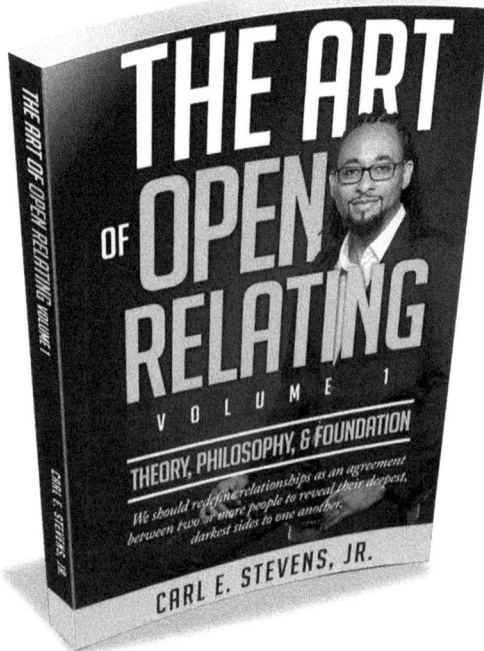

www.ingramcontent.com/pod-product-compliance
Lightning Source LLC
Chambersburg PA
CBHW052033090426
42739CB00010B/1891